# Divine Mercy
# for Moms

W9-CIB-228

*may mercy tranform you!*

Emily Jaminet

Michele Faehnle

"I hope you will read this book and help save the world. We need you, Catholic moms! From your often overlooked love, God will grant us extraordinary gifts of grace in the present time of mercy."

From the foreword by **Fr. Michael E. Gaitley, MIC**
Author of *33 Days to Morning Glory*

"*Divine Mercy for Moms* makes what's all-too-easily an abstract concept into a tangible approach. Roll up your sleeves and prepare to dog-ear your copy as your family life and personal devotion are challenged and enhanced."

**Sarah A. Reinhard**
Catholic blogger, speaker, writer,
and author of *A Catholic Mother's Companion to Pregnancy*

"*Divine Mercy for Moms* is profound yet simple, compelling yet gentle. Sharing their own lived experience, the authors testify to the transformative power of the devotion in their families and marriages with encouragement that is candid, wise, and very practical."

**Nancy and Patrick Madrid**
Radio host and author of *Why Be Catholic?*

"'Jesus, I trust in you!' Why is trust often such a stumbling block for today's busy moms? *Divine Mercy for Moms* invites us into a profound consideration of the life and spirituality of St. Faustina Kowalska from the vantage point of motherhood. We moms are often called to be angels of mercy in our home as we—often literally—commit ourselves to the corporal and spiritual works of mercy. And yet far too often, we neglect to appreciate that our home is our primary 'mercy mission field.' Let Michele and Emily introduce you to the beauty of St. Faustina's Divine Mercy devotion and help you bring this amazing spiritual gift to life in your home. Perfect for small groups and anyone looking to draw ever closer to Jesus Christ."

**Lisa M. Hendey**
Founder of *CatholicMom.com* and author of *The Grace of Yes*

"Through engaging stories and practical applications (good for any busy mom), Michele Faehnle and Emily Jaminet show how the simple, ordinary tasks of motherhood can have extraordinary results when done with a heart that knows the power of God's Divine Mercy. This book is a must read for any mom who has ever uttered the words, 'Lord, have mercy.'"

**Kelly Wahlquist**
Founder of Women In the New Evangelization and author of *Created to Relate*

Jesus, I trust in You

Scripture texts in this work are taken from the *New American Bible, Revised Edition* © 2010, 1991, 1986, 1970 Confraternity of Christian Doctrine, Washington, DC, and are used by permission of the copyright owner. All rights reserved. No part of the *New American Bible* may be reproduced in any form without permission in writing from the copyright owner.

Passages cited from the *Diary of St. Maria Faustina Kowalska: Divine Mercy in My Soul* © 1987 Marian Fathers of the Immaculate Conception of the B.V.M. All rights reserved. Used with permission.

© 2016 by Michele Faehnle and Emily Jaminet

Foreword © 2016 by Michael E. Gaitley, MIC

Afterword © 2016 by Lisa M. Hendey

All rights reserved. No part of this book may be used or reproduced in any manner whatsoever, except in the case of reprints in the context of reviews, without written permission from Ave Maria Press®, Inc., P.O. Box 428, Notre Dame, IN 46556, 1-800-282-1865.

Founded in 1865, Ave Maria Press is a ministry of the United States Province of Holy Cross.

www.avemariapress.com

Paperback: ISBN-13 978-1-59471-665-2

E-book: ISBN-13 978-1-59471-666-9

Cover image "Saint Mary Faustina Kowalska" © Ivona Staszewski, available on shop.evonagallery.com and www.etsy.com/shop/Evonagallery.

Cover and text design by Katherine Robinson.

Printed and bound in the United States of America.

*Library of Congress Cataloging-in-Publication Data is available.*

# Divine Mercy
# for Moms

Sharing the Lessons of St. Faustina

Foreword by Fr. Michael E. Gaitley, MIC
Afterword by Lisa M. Hendey

## MICHELE FAEHNLE
## EMILY JAMINET

AVE MARIA PRESS AVE Notre Dame, Indiana

# Contents

# Publisher's Note

Michele Faehnle and Emily Jaminet wrote this book as a joint project. They collaborated on the introduction, study guide, and appendixes. Michele penned chapters 1, 4, and 6; while Emily handled chapters 2, 3, and 5.

Quotations from St. Faustina's *Diary* follow a distinctive style: Plain text signifies Faustina's own thoughts, bold type indicates words she received from Jesus, and italics denote Mary's words to her. Parenthetical citations in this book refer to paragraph numbers from the *Diary*, rather than page numbers.

# Foreword

Now is the time of mercy! Now is a time of great and extraordinary grace for the Church and the world. This was the insight of St. John Paul II for our time, something that has been repeated by subsequent popes.

John Paul's insight came from his assessment of our modern world. Specifically, while he clearly recognized the blessings of technology and science, he also recognized that, in many ways, the times we're living in are marked by unprecedented evil. But for that very reason, the pope knew, God is also reaching out to our hurting, broken world, in a certain sense, more than ever.

One of the most powerful ways that God is reaching out to us is through the Divine Mercy message and devotion that comes to us from St. Faustina Kowalska, about whom you'll learn more in this book. Through her message, which reminds us that mercy is the central message of the Gospel, God seems to want to start a chain reaction. Having revealed his great mercy to us in a special way through the testimony of St. Faustina, though her, he wants to inspire countless more people to be living images of Divine Mercy.

In this book, Emily Jaminet and Michele Faehnle refer to a beautiful prayer of St. Faustina, "A Prayer of Transformation from Within." In this prayer, St. Faustina asks to be transformed into a living reflection of God's mercy, specifically praying that her eyes, ears, tongue, hands, feet, and heart be instruments of God's tender mercy. She essentially wants to be God's mercy for the world, to be a channel of Divine Mercy, a place through which God's mercy can pass through her heart and soul to everyone.

Now, we might ask, "Why did God put the desire of that prayer into St. Faustina's heart?" I believe he did so to reveal a key part of his strategy of bringing his gift of salvation to our world, in this present time of mercy. He wants to use not just Faustina but all of *us* as instruments of his mercy. More specifically, he wants to transform us into living images of Divine Mercy, so he can reach everyone with his tender love and save them.

But he's not looking for just anyone for this important mission. In fact, I believe that his first picks for this solemn mission, his desired "special ops," are those who are most forgotten, overlooked, and underappreciated—the ones who, in the eyes of the world, don't amount to much. And who are they?

Well, I would argue that some of those who are most overlooked by the world, the ones who the world tends to scoff at are *mothers*, especially stay-at-home moms. Really. Modern pagans often don't take motherhood as serious business. Of course, they probably recognize that it's necessary for continuing the species, but it seems that they see it as something like farming: a dirty, difficult job, that somebody's got to do—but who would want to? It requires an enormous amount of effort behind-the-scenes, lots of thankless self-sacrifice, and involves work that isn't very glamorous.

But you know what? What the world sees as unimportant is often most important to the Lord. And how important are mothers? Well, I believe that in this time of mercy, God wants to use them to save the world. I believe he wants to use such hidden souls to complete his strategy of bringing down mercy on humanity. How? Through their unseen merciful deeds, words, and prayers. So, for instance, they help save the world by praying the Chaplet of Divine Mercy while picking up kids from school, by making acts of trust in Jesus in the midst of trials and crosses, and by taking up mundane works of mercy for children and husbands who may never fully realize their sacrifices.

Now, while St. Faustina was not a mother in a physical sense, she was a powerful spiritual mother whose prayers and sacrifices gave birth to grace in souls. And how important was she? Well, Jesus said to her, "**For your sake, I withhold the hand that punishes; for your sake I bless the earth**" (431). And how important are you? Let me put it this way: If you live what's in this book, Jesus will likely say the same thing to you!

But you have to read the book. I mean, just as it takes special training to be transformed into a special ops soldier for one's country, so it also takes special training to be transformed into a special ops soldier of mercy for God.

This book provides such training. These authors have embraced and been deeply transformed by Divine Mercy. Believe me, I know. I knew both of them in college, and I can attest that Michele and Emily have been deeply and radically transformed by Divine Mercy! Moreover, they have a gift for sharing how the process works. Through relatable stories and very practical suggestions, they show the way to becoming a channel of God's mercy to our families, our country, and the world.

I hope you will read this book and help save the world. We need you, Catholic moms! From your often

overlooked love, God will grant us extraordinary gifts
of grace in the present time of mercy.

Fr. Michael E. Gaitley, MIC
Director of Formation
Marian Missionaries of Divine Mercy

# Introduction

**For the sake of His sorrowful Passion have mercy on us and on the whole world. (476)[1]**

Thousands of pilgrims to the National Shrine of the Divine Mercy in Stockbridge, Massachusetts, chanted all around me on Divine Mercy Sunday in 2014. The sun was high in the sky, and the mercy and love of God were palpable in the sunlight and in the voices filling the air. I (Michele) had always longed to visit the shrine, though I never thought I would get the chance. Yet there I was, thirty-five weeks pregnant and with my whole family; I had a hard time believing it was real.

I was a pilgrim like all the others, but the Marians of the Immaculate Conception had also invited me to share my testimony of mercy and trust in God in a talk to the faithful who gathered on this significant feast day. I stared across the field filled with a sea of people and thought, "Why me Lord? Why ask a simple mom to stand before all these people and share about your mercy?" After I spoke, I was interviewed on the Catholic cable network EWTN during the Divine Mercy

preshow about a special works of mercy project I had
undertaken for Fr. Michael Gaitley. It was a miracle that
I had been asked to be a part of this special occasion,
and an even bigger miracle that my family was with
me.

I had had to choose between hopping on a plane
and going by myself, or bringing the rest of my family (husband and three children) with me on a ten-
hour road trip from our home in Columbus, Ohio. I
knew what an amazing experience it would be for my
whole family to experience the shrine on such a holy
day—it was, as they say, the opportunity of a lifetime.
I decided we should make the road trip together and
pitched the idea to my husband. Matt is self-employed,
and he wasn't so sure that a week of unpaid vacation,
especially with a new baby coming so soon, was a good
idea. He also reminded me that our Catholic school's
tuition for the next year was due shortly, and we certainly didn't have any spare money lying around! I
told him that if God wanted us to go, he would make
it clear to us with a sign.

How could he argue with that?

The following evening, we attended an auction and
fundraiser at our children's school. As her donation to
the school, my mother-in-law had given us forty dollars with which to bid on something at the auction. I
used the money to purchase one ticket to the "school
tuition raffle," so called because the prize was exactly
that: a year's free tuition! If you know anything at all
about what it costs to send a kid to Catholic school
these days, you can imagine how many of those tickets
were sold.

At eight forty-five, the drawing was announced. The emcee cracked some jokes and shook a gift bag full of names, finally drawing one ticket from the bag. Looking out over the crowd, he announced that the winner of the raffle was . . . Matt and Michele Faehnle!

I was in shock, even though I had been praying for a sign. Sometimes God just has to knock me over to get my attention—he certainly got it that night. One look at Matt told me I wasn't the only one who had decoded the signal: my husband knew where we were headed on spring break.

After hearing of this and other experiences of God's mercy in my life, my dear priest friend Fr. Dennis told me, "You have got to write this all down! You can't make up stuff that is this good!" And so I began writing *Divine Mercy for Moms*. As I began to write, I started to understand the task God was asking me to do, and I recalled a particular passage in the Gospel of Luke "After this the Lord appointed seventy-two others whom he sent ahead of him in pairs to every town and place he intended to visit" (Lk 10:1). I knew I needed another foot soldier in the field of motherhood to help me carry out this task, so I was inspired to bring my dear friend Emily Jaminet into the project.

As I look back over my life, I can see that one of the greatest mercies God has placed in my life is Emily's friendship. She is also the perfect choice as coauthor because her life exemplifies mercy. She's the type of friend who would give you the shirt off her back if you needed it, no matter the cost to her. It never failed when I arrived at Emily's home to work on the manuscript of *Divine Mercy for Moms* that she was watching one of our friends' children so the mom could get something else done. It was a great witness of truly being merciful to others.

## Emily

I had always felt that Michele and I were called to work together on a project that would be deeply meaningful, mostly in our own lives, perhaps, but also for others. As Pope John Paul II said upon arriving at Fatima on May 12, 1982, on the first anniversary of the attempt on his life: "In the designs of Providence, there are no mere *coincidences.*"

Our lives have interwoven so much over the past twenty years that it's sometimes hard to believe. Michele met her husband at my wedding and became engaged on my one-year anniversary. She was my labor and delivery nurse for the birth of my third child, and I had the joy of hosting the baby shower for her first. The best combined memory we have is from 2011, when we had babies on the same day—a little over an hour apart, in hospital rooms just down the hall from each other.

Through it all, our faith has remained the most binding element of our friendship. Michele and I both work in women's ministry for our diocesan Catholic Women's Conference, and I aspire to help mothers live out their faith with my daily Catholic radio reflections "A Mother's Moment." It was at the inspiration of Divine Providence (with a little help from our editor, Heidi Hess Saxton) that we decided to embark on this process of writing our first book together. We hope this book awakens your soul to the mercy of God, inspiring you to express and reflect that mercy toward your neighbor.

## A Year of Mercy

As Michele and I were writing one day, my phone started exploding with texts and calls from my brother Chad. "Did you hear the big news?" he practically screamed in my ear. "Pope Francis just declared a 'Year of Mercy!'" This special or "extraordinary" jubilee would begin on the Feast of the Immaculate Conception, December 8, 2015. Pope Francis proclaimed:

> Dear brothers and sisters, I have thought about how the Church can make clear its mission of being a witness of mercy. It's a journey that starts with a spiritual conversion. For this reason I have decided to declare an Extraordinary Jubilee that has the mercy of God at its center. It will be a Holy Year of Mercy. . . . From this moment, we entrust this holy year to the Mother of Mercy, that she might turn her gaze upon us and watch over our journey.[2]

In writing this book, we are filled with hope and joy at being able to share those moments in our lives in which we have experienced God's mercy. Though these moments have certainly helped us to grow in our faith, we write to you not as "supermoms" with perfect kids, but as those who are still navigating the path of motherhood and sanctity. It is through our personal imperfections, and those of our families, that we have learned mercy. People always ask us, "How do you do it?" In sharing our stories of mercy, we want to give you some practical ways to implement mercy in your life as a mother.

One way we are guided as Catholics to live out mercy is through the corporal and spiritual works of mercy. In *Misericordiae Vultus* (The Face of Mercy) Pope Francis affirms our intuition that mercy should be our focus as mothers. These acts of mercy reawaken our conscience, which too often grows dull through our own self-sufficiency. The works of mercy let us enter more deeply into the heart of the Gospel, where the poor have a special experience of God's mercy. Pope Francis writes:

> Let us rediscover these corporal and spiritual works of mercy that Jesus first introduced in his preaching. We cannot escape these words of the Lord to us, and they will serve as the criteria upon which we will be judged: whether we have fed the hungry and given drink to the thirsty, welcomed the stranger and clothed the naked, or spent time with the sick and those in prison (cf. Mt 25:31–45). Moreover, we will be asked if we have helped others to escape the doubt that causes them to fall into despair; if we have fought to overcome the ignorance in which millions of people live, especially children trapped in poverty; if we have been close to the lonely and afflicted; if we have forgiven those who have offended us and have rejected all forms of anger and hate that lead to violence; if we have had the kind of patience God shows, who is so patient with us; and if we have commended our brothers and sisters to the Lord in prayer. In each of these "little ones," Christ himself is present. His flesh becomes visible in the flesh of the tortured, the crushed, the scourged, the malnourished, and the exiled . . . to be acknowledged, touched, and cared for by us. Let us not forget the words of St. John of the Cross: "as we prepare to leave this life, we will be judged on the basis of love."[3]

## *What Is "Divine Mercy"?*

Fr. Michael Gaitley, who shared with you his insights in the foreword of this book, writes that Divine Mercy is "a particular kind of love, a particular mode of love when it encounters suffering, poverty, brokenness, and sin. *Divine* mercy is when God's love meets us and helps us in the midst of our suffering and sin ... *every good we receive* is an expression of Divine Mercy."[4]

With eleven kids between us, Michele and I understand the realities of life and the difficulties of our vocations as wives and mothers. Ours is a vocation of service, and as our daily actions are filtered through the prayerful lens of Divine Mercy, our hearts grow softer and more compassionate, until they are more like Christ's. Michele and I have both had deep spiritual awakenings as we began to live with—to dwell within—the devotion to Divine Mercy. This book traces the steps of our journeys, so you can experience the Merciful Heart of Jesus just as we have.

Each chapter begins with a quotation from the *Diary of St. Maria Faustina Kowalska: Divine Mercy in My Soul* for reflection. St. Faustina was a young Polish nun who came to be known as the "Apostle of Divine Mercy." Although mostly uneducated, Faustina had a deep relationship with God and experienced extraordinary visions of Jesus in which he revealed his great desire that the world should know the fullness of his mercy. She recorded these revelations in her *Diary*, which has touched millions. These revelations are known as the message of Divine Mercy.

At the end of each chapter we offer suggestions for living out mercy in deed, word, or prayer as requested by Jesus of St. Faustina in the *Diary:* "**I am giving you**

**three ways of exercising mercy toward your neighbor: the first—by deed, the second—by word, the third— by prayer. In these three degrees is contained the fullness of mercy, and it is an unquestionable proof of love for Me. By this means a soul glorifies and pays reverence to My mercy"** (742).

At the end of the book we include study questions. We encourage you to read this book with your friends in small-group study. Michele and I have been part of the same faith-sharing group for over ten years now and know the importance of getting together with our other mom friends to support each other in growing in our faith and sharing it with our children. We also know that one of the biggest mercies for a mom is an evening out with friends!

It is our great hope that you will experience Divine Mercy in your life's journey so that you too can be transformed into an instrument of mercy for others. We are so glad you could join us as we continue on this path with St. Faustina, because as Pope Francis reminds us, "this is the age of mercy."[5]

# CHAPTER 1

# St. Faustina, Apostle of
## Divine Mercy

**How long shall I put up with you and how long will you keep putting Me off? (9)**

"Faustina, please," I (Michele) told the cab driver, pointing to a small picture of Jesus hanging from his rearview mirror as my friends and I clambered into the back seat.

He nodded.

I had traveled to Kraków, Poland, for a weekend trip during my college semester abroad at the Franciscan University of Gaming, Austria. Although I spoke no Polish, the cab driver knew from my request exactly where to take us. He knew I had come to visit the shrine of the great saint Sr. Maria Faustina Kowalska. She was

a young Polish religious sister who in the 1930s experienced extraordinary visions of Jesus and his mother.
Although Faustina was not very well known in the
United States at the time of my visit to Kraków, she
was widely celebrated in Poland.

Hanging from the cab's mirror was a distinctive
picture known as the Image of Divine Mercy; it was
painted at the direction of St. Faustina to portray Jesus
as she had seen him in her visions. Devotion to the
Image was already very popular among the Polish
people and in recent times has surged in popularity
in the United States, where the Image hangs in many
Catholic homes and parishes, especially on the Sunday
after Easter (Divine Mercy Sunday).

As the cab driver headed for the Shrine of The
Divine Mercy in Kraków-Łagiewniki, the monastery
of the Sisters of Our Lady of Mercy where Faustina had
once lived, I tried to soak in as much as I could through
the windows. He drove us through the streets of a cold,
dark city that had languished for many years behind
the Iron Curtain. I had spent the day before touring
the concentration camps at Auschwitz, and I was still
trying to process all I had witnessed there. Because of
my Polish heritage, this trip had deep personal signif-
icance to me and the entire semester studying abroad
was a time of great soul searching.

I am a cradle Catholic. My parents had a very
devout faith life, yet mine was still growing. My parents, along with fourteen years of Catholic schools,
had taught me the Faith that I knew was the truth—I
just wasn't quite ready to give up my "ways of the
world" yet.

I had agreed to attend Franciscan University—a small liberal arts college in Steubenville, Ohio, known for its orthodox teaching in the Catholic faith—in no small part because I was intrigued by their study abroad program. I wanted to have fun and be with my friends. I thought that allowing Jesus to be the king of my life was a ticket straight to the convent, and I wanted no part in that. I told Jesus I needed a few more years of enjoying myself and then I would be on the straight and narrow. I would later understand that the unsettled feeling inside of me was a call to a deeper relationship with him and that the only way to true peace was to place my full trust in him and to put my life in his hands.

Sisters wearing long black habits and black veils with protruding white bills welcomed us upon our arrival at the convent. Faustina had once worn a habit just like theirs, an outward symbol of the community's commitment to Christ. As they showed us the convent and the grounds, the nuns shared the story of Faustina's life with us, as well as some of the many miraculous stories of healing attributed to her intercession.

Just before three o'clock, they led us to a beautiful chapel with a wooden side altar, above which hangs the full-sized Divine Mercy Image: a painting of the risen Christ in a white robe, one hand raised in blessing and the other touching his heart. Two rays of light stream from Jesus's chest, one red and one white. Underneath the Image is written *Jezu ufam Tobie* ("Jesus, I trust in You"). St. Faustina directed an artist to paint the original image on a canvas exactly as Jesus had instructed in a vision, promising that many graces would be received through it.[1] Below the painting I

saw the small, white coffin that holds the tomb and
the relics of St. Faustina. Along the walls are displayed
hundreds of ornaments representing favors asked
and graces received by pilgrims who have visited the
shrine.

At three o'clock, all the sisters living in the convent
gathered in the chapel to pray together the Chaplet of
Divine Mercy to commemorate the hour of Christ's
death on the Cross. With rosary beads in one hand, the
sisters stretched their arms out as Our Lord did during
the crucifixion, joining Jesus in his suffering, and began
chanting a series of prayers in Polish:

> **For the sake of His sorrowful Passion have mercy
> on us and on the whole world.** (476)

This was a powerful moment for me—to witness
this well-known prayer right where it had originated
in that small convent. I prayed first for all the family
and friends I could think of. Then I began to pray about
my vocation in life. I so longed for God to speak to me
audibly, as he did to St. Faustina, or even to send me
a letter. Instead I read the words at the bottom of the
Image again and said them like I meant them:

"Jesus, I trust in you." As I placed my life in his
hands, I felt at peace.

Twenty years later as I write this book, I can see
clearly the graces that have flowed from this pilgrimage. It was during that semester abroad that I finally
accepted my faith as my own rather than my parents',
began seeking a real relationship with Jesus, and experienced his great mercy.

## St. Faustina Kowalska and Divine Mercy: A Short History

If you have never before heard of the Divine Mercy devotion or St. Faustina, you may be wondering what is so amazing about this little uneducated nun and why St. John Paul II named her the "Apostle of Divine Mercy" at her canonization in 2000, encouraging the faithful to read her *Diary* and proclaiming Divine Mercy Sunday as a universal feast.

What did the saintly pope see in this cloistered sister that many of her contemporaries did not? And what does her canonization say to us about the beautiful providence of God, whose timing is often so different from our own?

Sr. Maria Faustina was born Helen Kowalska in 1905 to a poor family in Głogowiec, Poland, the third of ten children. She was a very pious and prayerful young girl and had a special place in her heart for the sufferings of others.

Young Helen knew she was called to religious life as early as age seven. She grew in holiness despite the fact she couldn't always attend Sunday Mass; the family only owned one Sunday dress, which was shared by the girls. Helen learned to read and write from her father and later went to school. Although she was a good student, she was forced to leave school after only two years to make room for younger students. At fourteen she moved in with another family to become a domestic servant. It was there she received a vision of a bright light and felt called to join the convent.

Her parents at first did not want her to join the convent, so she went back to work as a housekeeper. But

Jesus was persistent in his call: when she was eighteen, Helen experienced a vision of Jesus, who asked of her **"How long shall I put up with you and how long will you keep putting Me off?"** (9). After being refused by several orders, Helen was accepted into the Congregation of the Sisters of Our Lady of Mercy in Warsaw in 1925; it was then that she took her religious name: Sr. Maria Faustina of the Most Blessed Sacrament.

Initially she felt called to leave this order to join a stricter order, but Jesus made it clear to her that she was where he wanted her to be. Faustina made her vows with the Sisters of Our Lady of Mercy and served as a cook, gardener, and doorkeeper. She stayed in several different convents, but mainly at the convents in Kraków, Płock, and Wilno (now Vilnius, capital of Lithuania). During much of her life in the convent she was in ill health, as she suffered from tuberculosis, a terrible disease of the lungs. However she never complained about her suffering, instead offering it to Jesus for the poor souls in purgatory. She had a very meek and humble manner, and the sisters described her as always having "childlike joy on her face."[2]

In 1931, she was staying at the convent in Vilnius when she received the vision of Jesus as described above. Jesus instructed her to have him painted as she saw him and to see that the portrait was spread around the world.[3] When she first reported this request to her confessor, he told Faustina that Jesus just wanted her to paint his image in her soul. However, in another vision Jesus confirmed that he wanted a material image created.

Faustina asked a sister in the convent to paint the likeness for her. This sister declined, but word spread around the convent that Faustina was receiving visions. While a few of the sisters believed in her extraordinary experiences, St. Faustina wrote in the *Diary* that many "began to speak openly about me and to regard me as a hysteric and a fantasist, and the rumors began to grow louder" (125). Some of the sisters were very cruel and humiliated her publicly, but Faustina kept her peace and never uttered anything in her defense. She was soon blessed with a spiritual advisor, Fr. Michael Sopoćko, who would help her fulfill her mission.

After a doctor evaluated Faustina's physical and mental health and vouched for her sanity, Fr. Sopoćko helped find an artist, Eugeniusz Kazimirowski, to paint the picture under Faustina's direction. She visited the artist each weekend to instruct him and was dissatisfied with his first efforts. The painting was changed several times by Kazimirowski. In 1934, the painting was almost finished, but Sr. Faustina was still not pleased. She went to the chapel and cried. "Who will paint You as beautiful as You are?" she asked Jesus. In response she heard, **"Not in the beauty of the color, nor of the brush lies the greatness of this image, but in My grace"** (313). Sr. Faustina accepted the painting, saying, "It is not what it should be, but that's how it must remain."[4] The Divine Mercy Image was first displayed publicly on the Friday after Easter in 1935 at the Shrine of Our Lady of Ostra Brama in Vilnius, where Fr. Sopoćko gave a sermon about Divine Mercy. While he was preaching, Sr. Faustina saw the Image come alive, and the "rays pierced the hearts of the people gathered there"(417).

Jesus continued to appear to St. Faustina and reveal his mission for her to spread the message of his mercy throughout the world. There were no external signs of her great mysticism; she was obedient and cheerful and did her daily tasks with great love. St. Faustina also suffered greatly. She underwent a great "dark night of the soul," a deep spiritual pain experienced by some as they grow in spiritual maturity and union with God. What we know of her experiences is recorded in her *Diary*, which she continued to write until she died in 1938 from tuberculosis. She was only thirty-three.[5]

## Spreading the Message

Today Faustina's message of God's mercy and love continues to spread throughout the world, especially through the *Diary* in which she recorded over six hundred pages of revelations. It has sold almost a million copies to date. The essence of the message is that we should receive and trust in God's mercy and give mercifully to our neighbors.

The message of Divine Mercy is a private revelation, distinct from the public revelation gathered in Holy Scripture and Sacred Tradition and from the dogmas of the Church that derive from Holy Scripture. This means that the communications from Jesus and Mary that Faustina recorded in her *Diary* are not binding on believers (CCC 67). And yet, throughout the ages God has sent us prophets and mystics to give timely messages to our world that has forgotten his love. We can see many examples of prophets in the Old Testament and can look to John the Baptist in the New Testament. Jesus called his Apostles and other disciples during his lifetime and sent them out, and God continues to give us great and holy men and women to strengthen our Church. In declaring Faustina a saint, the Church affirmed that her life and her writing are consistent with the Gospel; by declaring Divine Mercy Sunday, St. John Paul II "baptized" the message of Divine Mercy and its Image as a trustworthy source of grace to be shared with the world.

The message of Divine Mercy is certainly needed during our time, and the last three popes have placed great emphasis on mercy as well as the devotion to Divine Mercy. St. John Paul II especially stressed the importance of this devotion to him personally and to our Church. He called the *Diary* "a particular Gospel of Divine Mercy written from a twentieth-century perspective."[6]

In his Regina Caeli Address for Divine Mercy in 2006, Pope Benedict XVI said that "Divine Mercy is not a secondary devotion, but an integral dimension of a Christian's faith and prayer."[7]

Pope Francis has continued to spread the message. He emphasizes that in our wounded world we need mercy, which allows people to experience the truth about God—that through this experience of mercy, the world will receive healing and conversion. In his first Angelus address Pope Francis proclaimed that mercy "is the best thing we can feel: it changes the world."[8]

Experiencing Divine Mercy has certainly transformed my life. The mercies I have received have helped me understand how to be more loving and more compassionate and have opened my eyes to the sufferings of others. As I have learned more about St. Faustina's childlike trust in God and her desire to grow in holiness by being merciful to her neighbor, I have grown in my desire to be an active witness of mercy.

## Respond to God's Call in Deed, Word, and Prayer

*Deed:* Is the story of St. Faustina new to you? Consider reading a story about her with your children, and have them draw their own version of the Image. Links to free resources can be found on divinemercyformoms. com. Alternatively, get a copy of the Image from your local Catholic bookstore or online to display in your home. For beautiful images on a budget, visit www. divinemercyart.org.

*Word:* This week, make a phone call or send a text message to a friend in need. Share God's mercy with the person; you may even incorporate a message from the *Diary* or from Scripture. For example:

*From your heart:* "I'm thinking of you and praying for you."

*From the Diary:* "**Before I made the world, I loved you with the love your heart is experiencing today and, throughout the centuries, My love will never change**" (1754).

*Prayer:* One of our favorite passages from the *Diary* is a prayer in the "General Exercises" section. If you are ready for Divine Mercy to change you, we invite you join us in prayer with these words of St. Faustina:

**St. Faustina's Prayer for Divine Transformation from Within** (163)[9]

+ O Most Holy Trinity! . . . I want to be completely transformed into Your mercy and to be Your living reflection, O Lord. . . .

Help me, O Lord, that my eyes may be merciful, so that I may never suspect or judge from appearances, but look for what is beautiful in my neighbors' souls and come to their rescue.

Help me, that my ears may be merciful, so that I may give heed to my neighbors' needs and not be indifferent to their pains and moanings.

Help me, O Lord, that my tongue may be merciful, so that I should never speak negatively of my neighbor, but have a word of comfort and forgiveness for all.

Help me, O Lord, that my hands may be merciful and filled with good deeds, so that I may do only good to my neighbors and take upon myself the more difficult and toilsome tasks.

Help me, that my feet may be merciful, so that I may hurry to assist my neighbor, overcoming my own fatigue and weariness. My true rest is in the service of my neighbor.

Help me, O Lord, that my heart may be merciful so that I myself may feel all the sufferings of my neighbor. . . . May Your mercy, O Lord, rest upon me.

# CHAPTER 2

# Developing Trust in Jesus through the *Divine Mercy* Devotion

**Encourage the souls with whom you come in contact to trust in My infinite mercy. Oh, how I love those souls who have complete confidence in Me—I will do everything for them. (294)**

"For my thoughts are not your thoughts, nor are your ways my ways," says the Lord (Is 55:8). This is the first lesson we learn from the life of Sr. Faustina. God chose this simple country girl to deliver the most important message of our era. She not only lived this message, but promoted it to the whole world from her quiet life in a convent.

Her *Diary* reveals how Christ led Faustina each step of the way to accomplish this awesome mission. Yet this great saint did many ordinary jobs that are much like the many roles of mothers. She was a childcare provider and a live-in nanny and worked at a bakery shop and a retail store. Later she attended to the convent door and was the convent gardener. Her jobs required no extensive training or special talent, but each person who met her knew of her gentle and kind ways and commented on her handwork and authentic faith.

This simple nun had a tremendous responsibility: **"You will prepare the world for My final coming"** (429). What a task! Jesus also told her, **"In the Old Covenant I sent prophets wielding thunderbolts to My people. Today I am sending you with My mercy to the people of the whole world"** (1588). This mission does not end with St. Faustina; Christ is calling all of us to bring God's mercy to others.

St. Faustina was not only a great mystic, but also a true prophet. When one of her religious sisters expressed disappointed that their convent chapel was open only to the sisters of their congregation, Faustina told Mother Superior, "There will soon come a time when the convent gate will be wide open and people will come here to pray to the Divine Mercy."[1] She knew that the nuns' humble chapel would one day become the shrine for the worship of the Divine Mercy.

I (Emily) experienced the prophetic nature of her words a few months before Michele, when I too traveled across Europe during college. Of all the places I visited, the one that would most profoundly affect my life was that same tiny chapel in Kraków-Łagiewniki,

Poland. I am still amazed that, as a simple college student, I not only had heard of Sr. Faustina (who was beatified but not yet canonized at the time), but made a point to visit her convent. My experience there inspired me to join in the mission to promote this devotion and live out St. Faustina's spirituality.

The gospel call to mercy is timeless and necessary. As a young mother pregnant with my second child, I traveled to the Holy Land during the Great Jubilee of the Year 2000 and was able to pray on the hill where Christ delivered the Sermon on the Mount. As I slowly climbed the embankment of that hill, I envisioned myself as one of the more than five thousand people who originally heard Jesus proclaim this key gospel teaching. Jesus established clearly that mercy is at the center of our Christian faith.

The Divine Mercy message reinforces the fifth Beatitude: "Blessed are the merciful, for they will be shown mercy" (Mt 5:7) or "Be merciful, just as your Father is merciful" (Lk 6:36). In this Beatitude, Jesus gives holiness a new emphasis, expressing it as "mercy that reaches out to others and no longer divides people into segregated camps or disqualifies some and not others to enter the family of God."[2] God's mercy is for everyone, for Christ came to share with us his new kingdom, the kingdom of mercy.

Christ is calling all of us to be people of Divine Mercy and to place our trust in him. The more we turn to Christ with our hearts and strive to trust his will in our lives, the more we will receive the graces we need to live out our vocations as wives and mothers. Divine Mercy is not just a devotion, but a lifestyle we can depend on as mothers. Christ calls each of us to receive his Divine Mercy—and then to live it out and to pass it on to others.

St. Faustina brings this message to life as she opens her heart and soul through her *Diary* for all generations, sharing with us her deep and personal relationship with Jesus Christ and the message about his mercy that he wants her to spread. In her inspirational diary, Jesus Christ comes alive as if he is speaking to us directly.

In the introduction of her *Diary* (xix–xxv), St. Faustina shares with us five elements of the Divine Mercy devotion that will help us mothers receive powerful graces from Jesus and, in return, show mercy to others:

1. The Image of Divine Mercy
2. The Feast of Divine Mercy
3. The Chaplet of Divine Mercy
4. The Hour of Great Mercy
5. Spreading devotion to Divine Mercy

These engaging invitations to meditation, prayer, and action will help us better live out our vocations as wives and mothers. Motherhood is a vocation of service and constant love. We can weave these five practices into our daily lives so that we can be vessels for the Lord. Let's explore them now.

## 1. The Image of Divine Mercy

Jesus said to me, **Paint an image according to the pattern you see, with the signature: Jesus, I trust**

**in You. . . . I want this image . . . to be solemnly
blessed.** (47, 49)

Just think, Jesus had a personal portrait painted of him
so that we could visualize Divine Mercy. He gave us
a "selfie"!

Mothers need visuals. It is not enough for us to hear
or read that God loves us; we must also have a familiar,
loving face on which our eyes can rest. Research has
shown that we remember visual images much better
and more easily than we do words.[3] I found this to be
true when I launched into motherhood in my early
twenties, dealing with a colicky baby. I needed a way to
visualize Christ's compassion for me and my little one
as I was called to tend to the child with Christ's own
tenderness and kindheartedness, despite the screaming
day and night. The Divine Mercy message is not just
words; Christ provides us with a picture of what mercy
looks like, one upon which we can reflect and gain
strength. He is mercy and offers mercy if we accept it.

On my phone alone I have more than a thousand
pictures. I love to scroll back through the pictures and
revisit the many memories I have of my family—the
happy memories and even the not-so-happy ones.
Christ gave us a beautiful visual to remind us of his
love and mercy. He wants us to remember him as the
risen Lord, not only on the Cross suffering. He wants
us to turn our eyes to this Image and the rays flowing
from his heart so we understand that he is offering his
love and mercy to us.

Focusing on the rays is powerful because they sig-
nify the water and the blood that poured forth from

Christ's heart through his pierced side at the crucifixion (Jn 19:34):

> **The pale ray stands for the Water which makes souls righteous. The red ray stands for the Blood which is the life of souls. . . . Happy is the one who will dwell in their shelter.** (299)

These rays give us mothers hope and healing. They symbolize the sacraments of Baptism and Reconciliation as well as the Eucharist. Hope and healing are a constant need for mothers, as we can be plagued with guilt and remorse over our failures, no matter how hard we try to raise our children well and do what we think is right in the moment. In our constant striving to do better, to improve our ways, we can lose sight of our need to trust in the Lord. The rays that flow out of Christ's heart are a graphic reminder of his mercy and his love for us.

My favorite aspect of the Image is that in it Christ is walking toward us. If you look carefully, you will note that Jesus's left foot is stepping forward. He gazes downward, as if from the Cross. He is always walking toward us in love; he wants us to know that his mercy is for us personally. He not only wants to walk *with* us, he is walking *toward* us, calling for us to trust in him. The words "Jesus, I trust in you" should be written on our hearts.

In order to give mercy, we too must be willing to step toward those around us, whether they are members of our family or others. As we strive to meet people where they are in life, it is important to remember that we are all on our own individual spiritual journeys, so we must show others love and kindness and not judge them.

When we bring religious items into our homes, we not only share our faith with our family but can receive actual graces. Many graces are promised to those who look upon the Image and have one in their homes, such as the promise that souls will not perish, that they will have victory over enemies on earth, and that Jesus himself will defend souls who venerate the image as his own glory.[4]

These promises may seem strange to the modern ear, but I know of many stories of peace brought into families' homes, protection of their property and family, even miraculous healings! The Image of Divine Mercy helps inspire us to trust Jesus, and this trust brings us the graces that are promised as we allow him to work miracles of mercy in our hearts. By inviting Jesus into our homes with this image, we are reminded each day that we have invited him into the life of our family. Motherhood stretches our hearts; the Image can help us to connect with our Lord in our daily lives. We are capable of so much more with Christ strengthening us.

## 2. The Feast of Divine Mercy

**I desire that there be a Feast of Mercy . . . on the first Sunday after Easter.** (49)

Divine Mercy Sunday, the Sunday after Easter, is a Catholic parent's dream. The simple words "Jesus, I trust in you" convey an orientation of heart that Jesus wants us all to have, which is why he asked St. Faustina to have the phrase written at the bottom of the Divine

Mercy Image. These words can be the foundation of our lives if we embrace them.

Jesus promised to **"pour out a whole ocean of graces upon those souls who approach the Fount of My Mercy"** (699) on this day. To celebrate this great feast day and receive the promised graces of complete forgiveness of sins and the punishment associated with those sins (699) is actually pretty easy—go to confession before or on the feast, attend Mass in the state of grace and receive Communion with the intention of receiving the graces, and do an act of mercy.[5]

At the canonization of St. Faustina in 2000, the future saint Pope John Paul II proclaimed the first Sunday after Easter "Divine Mercy Sunday," to be universally recognized by the Church from that day forward. This day was so special to this pope that he told Dr. Valentin Fuster, the cardiologist who investigated the miracle that led to St. Faustina's canonization, "This is the happiest day of my life."[6] As renowned author and speaker on Divine Mercy Fr. Michael Gaitley writes, "It is a day of extraordinary grace of being cleansed of sin and punishment due to sin."[7] Today, many parishes offer special celebrations on Divine Mercy Sunday to make it easy for you to go to confession, attend Mass, and even do your act of mercy by praying the Chaplet for others. I never miss this special feast day. Even before it was officially proclaimed I would seek out a parish hosting this devotion because of the great graces I knew I would receive.

To prepare for the feast, our family prays the Divine Mercy Novena, which starts on Good Friday and ends on Divine Mercy Sunday. The whole family enjoys this simple and powerful devotion. We also bring out the

Divine Mercy Image and place it on our mantel so we can focus on Christ's mercy as we contemplate the Passion, death, and Resurrection of our Lord Jesus during the Easter Triduum and the following week leading up to Divine Mercy Sunday.

## 3. The Chaplet of Divine Mercy

**Say unceasingly the chaplet that I have taught you.** (687)

Jesus asked St. Faustina to pray these specific prayers on rosary beads:

**First of all, you will say one Our Father and Hail Mary and the I believe in God. Then on the Our Father bead you will say the following words: "Eternal Father, I offer You the Body and Blood, Soul and Divinity of Your dearly beloved Son, Our Lord Jesus Christ, in atonement for our sins and those of the whole world." On the Hail Mary beads you will say the following words: "For the sake of His sorrowful Passion have mercy on us and on the whole world." In conclusion, three times you will recite these words: "Holy God, Holy Mighty One, Holy Immortal One, have mercy on us and on the whole world." (476)**

This simple rhythmic prayer is so easy to pray that my children were able to memorize the words at the age of two. My children find this devotion attractive because it requires only a small amount of time, which is helpful for their short attention spans. We gather as a family in the car or at home to join together in prayer. Teaching children to "pause and pray" is a great way not only to build their faith but also to help them see Christ as merciful and trustworthy.

The Chaplet also holds special graces for those who are dying. Jesus promised St. Faustina the following if it is prayed in the presence of someone who is dying: **"When they say this chaplet in the presence of the dying, I will stand between My Father and the dying person, not as the just Judge but as the merciful Savior"** (1541).

Michele shared with me a very powerful story surrounding the death of her husband's grandfather. Knowing the promise of the Chaplet, she headed with her family to the nursing home so that they could pray it at his bedside. However, because of some treatments Grandpa was receiving, the family were unable to stay for very long, so they a left a pamphlet containing instructions on how to pray the Chaplet on the bedside table. Michele's family prayed the Chaplet for him in the car on the way home. That evening, another family member, who had never prayed the Chaplet before, decided to pray it with the help of the pamphlet before she left the nursing home. She prayed not only the Chaplet, but a sort of super-Chaplet: on each bead of her rosary, she prayed both the Rosary prayers and the Chaplet prayers aloud, so Grandpa could hear and be comforted by the words. Shortly after she finished, Grandpa breathed his last breath peacefully. The family believes it was because Jesus and Our Lady were there with him.

Many priests share that the dying people they visit are often agitated, but when the priests pray the Chaplet at the bedside they often see them go into a state of peace before death.

The Chaplet of Divine Mercy is a great devotion for the whole family. It is a prayer that can complement the Rosary or other devotions or be said on its own. Not only is this prayer easy to pray, but its simplicity makes it very easy to teach other people and to promote. The Chaplet is also beautiful if it is sung or chanted. The simple words make it easy for anyone to learn and join in the prayer.

As we live out the vocation of motherhood, we can reach out to the heavenly Father in prayer and ask for the graces we need to be holy. Graces are like specific gifts for the soul to strengthen us to better live out our vocations. St. Faustina shares with us over and over again that the Chaplet is worth praying. **"There are few souls who contemplate My Passion with true feeling; I give great graces to souls who meditate devoutly on My Passion"** (737). Besides praying for the graces we need, when we invoke "mercy on us and on the whole world," we do a powerful act of mercy by praying for the whole world.

## 4. The Hour of Great Mercy

**My daughter, . . . as often as you hear the clock strike the third hour, immerse yourself completely in My mercy, adoring and glorifying it; invoke its omnipotence for the whole world, and particularly for poor sinners; for at that moment mercy was opened wide for every soul.** (1572)

The gospels report that Jesus died on the Cross at three o'clock in the afternoon (Mt 27:46–50; Mk 15:34–37). St. Faustina's *Diary* has three specific recommendations for prayers being offered during the three o'clock hour:

1.  They need to be addressed to Jesus.
2.  They need to be said at three o'clock in the afternoon.
3.  They are to appeal to the value and merits of Christ's Passion.[8]

As the mother of seven children, I (Emily) know how hard it can be to take time out and reflect on the important things in life. Moms seem always to be running between school, sports, activities, and (for many of us) work, and let's not forget the never-ending duties of the house. At three o'clock, I am ready for either another cup of coffee or a nap to recharge me for the rest of my day, but the fact is that the day is just picking up. Three o'clock in the afternoon is the transition time in our house, the hour when school kids arrive home and the family gathers together again after a long day.

I have found that, instead of concentrating on myself and getting distracted by my children at this time, I am better off putting Christ first. If I pause to think about Christ and what he did for me, the rest of the day will go according to his plan, which is far better than any I could formulate on my own. This three o'clock hour is holy, and our Lord wants us to take time out of our busy lives to remember his Passion. Just like our children, who need constant reminders regarding the tasks they need to complete, we can benefit from this reminder from heaven.

This devotion is very practical. The three o'clock hour is about offering up our lives to Jesus. If you are fortunate enough to be able to sneak away, St.

Faustina suggests praying the Stations of the Cross or visiting the Blessed Sacrament. However, she also records the words of Jesus, who says, **"should you be unable to step into the chapel, immerse yourself in prayer there where you happen to be, if only for a very brief instant"** (1572). Even if we can't make it to a holy place, we can offer up all our tasks and unite them with Christ's suffering on the Cross. This simple act of prayer and refocusing on what is important will refresh our hearts and give us the right perspective to enjoy the remainder of the day.

I have come to realize that consistent prayer is important; it is not something I can put off until life slows down. I was especially guilty of neglecting regular prayer while my first three children were young. I would wait for a quiet time to pray instead of allowing my contemplation to take place in union with my vocation. I wasted a lot of time feeling frustrated with my vocation. Sadly, instead of asking Christ to join me on my radical ride of motherhood, I felt that motherhood was holding me back from growing spiritually. Now, I try to unite my vocation as a wife and mother with prayer. I soon discovered that each moment I gave to Christ with intentionality and love, I received not only the graces I needed to be a good mother, but true happiness as well.

Jesus said to St. Faustina, **"With childlike simplicity talk to Me about everything, for My ears and heart are inclined towards you, and your words are dear to Me"** (921). Christ is offering us a personal relationship with him. We can begin with knowing that we are his daughters and he wants us to come to him. Go to him and lay your burdens down no matter what is on your mind. When three o'clock strikes, you may be in the midst of performing your motherly duties or completing tasks at work, but if you turn your thoughts toward Christ even for a moment, tell him what is on your heart, and listen, you will be richly blessed.

In the *Diary*, Jesus shares this with Sr. Faustina: **"Oh, if souls would only want to listen to My voice when I am speaking in the depths of their hearts, they would reach the peak of holiness in a short time"** (584). Prayer is a two-way conversation with God. There is nothing worse than a friend who always talks and never listens. Provide Christ opportunities to speak to your heart and instruct you. He is oftentimes very creative about how he reaches out to us; sometimes it is through the mouths of our children. The other day my daughter got in the car after school and said, "Put your chatterbox down, Mom!" She was right: I needed to put my phone down and give my attention to my children.

When the stress of parenting creeps in late in the afternoon, pray the Chaplet in your head, even if the kids are melting down! Let Jesus help you! These powerful words can carry you through a nerve-racking moment. And by simply trusting in Christ, we will be able to handle our daily stresses better, determine how to live out God's will, and invoke grace for poor sinners. I am certain that prayer is the key to finding inner peace and living out this devotion.

## 5. Spreading Devotion to Divine Mercy

**Souls who spread the honor of My mercy I shield through their entire lives as a tender mother her infant.** (1075)

The Divine Mercy devotion is one that is not only worth living, but worth spreading to others—first and foremost, to our own families. It is practical and easy for mothers to promote and live out. As discussed earlier, Christ offers us a "selfie," a special feast day, quick prayers that are easy to remember, a specific daily hour for prayer, and an action plan to go out and promote the devotion. This is the perfect tailor-made plan for busy mothers in this modern era, since we love to know what we are supposed to do next.

One day while I was driving down the road, my two-year-old asked to lead the Divine Mercy Chaplet! All of a sudden, he began with "sake of His sorrowful Passion." I had never officially taught him the prayers; his presence during prayer times had been enough. Teaching children to pray takes effort, especially if it is new to you, but this small step of having your young children present during family prayer time can serve as a true witness and begin teaching them the Faith.

Family prayer is an opportunity to bring the family together. Sometimes we need to adjust our expectations and realize that family prayer is about family unity with God, not necessarily about successful completion of a task. As Catholics we have access to a vast number of prayers and devotions that we can pray together. Family prayer might not seem fruitful for you, but it has a different purpose from that of personal prayer time: promoting family unity and teaching the invaluable habit of prayer. Family prayer time does not replace your personal prayer time. In the past, our family has endured some very difficult "prayer gatherings" with our kids acting crazy: toddlers running around and babies crying. Now, with a house full of teens, we have other issues—kids grumbling about praying and sometimes starting to micromanage their younger siblings. No matter what ages your children are, you will find challenges to praying as a family. Just keep trying!

When children understand how important prayer is, they come to appreciate why we do it. Family prayer time needn't be stressful to us if we approach it as we do taking on any new habit—with the understanding that it will require patience. Move slowly and set your sights on your end goal, which is family unity with Christ.

"The spreading of the honor of the Divine Mercy does not require many words but always the Christian attitude of faith, of trust in God, and of becoming ever more merciful. Christ wants those who worship Him to perform at least one act of love of neighbor in the course of each day."[9] Christ is calling us to have the lenses we need to see others' sufferings and be his hands and feet to serve them. Motherhood is all about service and love toward others, resulting in the perfect training for action outside of family life.

If we unite our service to others with our love for God it will be easy for us to do a merciful deed each day! The key to doing a merciful deed is to keep our eyes open for opportunities to serve others. It doesn't need to be dramatic, but rather, we need to allow the Holy Spirit to show us what we are called to do. As women, we can use our maternal instinct to detect those around us who are in need of love and mercy. When we show others mercy we not only teach our children to serve, but we ourselves grow in holiness.

Living out the essential elements of Divine Mercy—meditating on the Divine Mercy Image, receiving the graces offered during Divine Mercy Sunday, praying the Chaplet, praying during the three o'clock hour, and spreading the devotion—will help us become extraordinary mothers and daughters of God. The key to the whole devotion rests at the bottom of the Image: "Jesus, I trust in you."

### Respond to God's Call in Deed, Word, and Prayer

*Deed:* Set your timer each day this week to go off at three o'clock in the afternoon. Wherever you are, take a moment to be still and turn your heart toward the Lord. Pray, "Jesus, I trust in you!"

*Word:* Share one aspect of the Divine Mercy devotion with a family member or friend. A great quick resource is the Divine Mercy App from the Association of Marian Helpers http://www.thedivinemercy.org/app/

*Prayer:* Take a few minutes to pray the Chaplet of Divine Mercy. If you are short on time, just do one decade. See Appendix 1 for step-by-step directions if you are not familiar with the prayer.

# CHAPTER 3

# Showing Mercy to Our Neighbor

**I am giving you three ways of exercising mercy toward your neighbor: the first—by deed, the second—by word, the third—by prayer. In these three degrees is contained the fullness of mercy, and it is an unquestionable proof of love for Me. . . . By means of this image I shall grant many graces to souls. It is to be a reminder of the demands of My mercy, because even the strongest faith is of no avail without works. (742)**

When my husband and I (Emily) were first married, we would commute into downtown Pittsburgh together each morning. Early one spring day, after we passed through the tunnel and over the bridge that marked the entrance to the city, we came to a stop at a particularly

busy merge point. While we sat there, I spied a homeless man bedded down in the grassy area between the
congested on and off ramps. He must have crossed
over in the middle of the night while traffic was light
but now was surrounded on all sides by moving cars!

I can still envision his blue sleeping bag, his ratty
old coat, the backpack by his side, and, despite the
relatively warm morning, the ski cap atop his head.
Seeing him trapped there, I felt moved to help him. I
looked down, saw my brown bag lunch, and thought
about how hungry he must be after a night of sleeping
outside. Without further reflection, I leaned out the
passenger window, screamed "Hey!" and hurled the
sack with all my might over the roof of the car toward
the man. My lunch flew through the air, and to my
everlasting horror I watched my apple and yogurt con-
tainer separate from the bag and strike the man like a
shotgun burst just before he was able to raise his arm
to block my "merciful offering." He dropped behind
a mound of shrubs as the traffic in front of us began
to move.

Red-faced, I dropped back into my seat and glanced
at my husband, who looked at me incredulously, his
mouth hanging open. "Well, *that* didn't go as planned,"
I murmured lamely.

To this day, I prefer not to imagine what that poor
man must have thought of me, not to mention all
those in nearby cars who witnessed what must have
looked like an attack on a homeless man. Though my
intentions were pure and rooted in a desire to help,
my impetuous act wounded, rather than elevated, the
dignity of the man I wanted to help.

# Three Ways of Exercising Mercy

While this particular example tends toward the extreme, we have all had moments in our lives in which we acted without exercising proper prudence. Perhaps we agreed to take on more activities or responsibilities than we should have in the name of serving others, only to find that the new activities added a great deal of stress to our family by hindering our ability to serve our loved ones. Or maybe we allowed ourselves to fall into inaction for fear of saying the wrong thing to someone in pain. Whatever the case, our intentions are often pure and rooted in love. Faustina says in her *Diary*, "Jesus, You have given me to know and understand in what a soul's greatness consists: not in great deeds but in great love. Love has its worth, and it confers greatness on all our deeds. Although our actions are small and ordinary in themselves, because of love they become great and powerful before God" (889).

As mothers, we have a powerful tool to help us figure out how to live lives of mercy in our homes. That tool is the love of God, the very flame that ignites our hearts and sustains us. Love is something that is limitless, we can never "love too much." The good news is that we can ask the Lord day in and day out to sanctify our hearts so that we always have more love! Our success as wives and mothers is dependent on God's love working constantly in our hearts, so that we can love our families through the service required by our vocations.

As Christians, we come to learn that we need to extend mercy not only to others, but to ourselves. We need to take time out to forgive ourselves for our own shortcomings, and recognize our littleness as mothers. Motherhood is humbling and challenging at times. We are tossed into a vocation with no manual, and a great calling to love unconditionally just like Christ loves us. Our goal is to do the will of God and be people who show love and mercy to others, and this includes ourselves. As mothers there are occasions when we will let others and ourselves down by not doing the right thing, saying the right thing or praying for those we want to pray for. When these moments happen, we need to remember that Christ is constantly there for us, offering us love and forgiveness. When we humbly turn to him, we experience a new freedom and joy that only God can give.

Thanks to the Divine Mercy message, we now have a plan for acting in mercy. We know to order our actions following a threefold formula—deed, word, and prayer. This formula, which Jesus gave to St. Faustina, can be explained simply.

1. When we see someone suffering, we are first to reach out to them with a *deed* of mercy. So in my example above—after learning some prudence—I call the man over and hand him my lunch with a smile.

2. If I am unable to stop when I see someone asking for food, or don't have anything to give, I can offer a *word*; saying or writing something that helps lessen the suffering of the person is what Jesus directs us to next. I acknowledge the person's presence with a look in the eye, a smile, or a simple "God bless you."

3. Finally, if I am unable to do a deed or communicate a word, I can always offer a *prayer*. I ask God to be with this suffering person in a special way.

## Be Not Afraid—Mercy Multiplies

St. John Paul II calls us to "Be not afraid." We must not be timid or fearful of living a life of Divine Mercy. If we believe, after a moment of reflection and prayer, that the Holy Spirit is prompting us to do something, then we must not be afraid to act, trusting that God will use our sometimes flawed human actions and work through us. Our yes to God is a yes to others, and from that yes miracles can happen.

Does that unnerve you, the thought that God might work a miracle or change the course of a life through you? That's where the "be not afraid" comes in. "For human beings this is impossible, but for God all things are possible" (Mt 19:26).

In life we can think that our actions are imprudent, but in fact the Lord might be asking a mighty deed of us. Think of Noah building an ark large enough to carry his family and two of every kind of animal safely through the flood (see Gen 7–8). Remember the little boy who shared his lunch with Jesus . . . who blessed it and fed thousands of people with it (see Mk 6:34–44). When we step out and try to follow God's lead, he will reward that trusting obedience—though we may not see all the ways the Lord uses us to accomplish his purposes in this lifetime.

Once while I was attending a wedding shower, I asked the bride-to-be about her plans for her wedding cake. She confided in me about how expensive wedding cakes were and how they might not even have enough cake for all the guests.

The words were out of my mouth before I could stop them: "Well then, I will make all the cakes for the wedding." The bride happily accepted . . . and soon I was kicking myself. How on earth was I going to make enough cake for *two hundred people?!*

The wedding was about six weeks before my sixth baby was due, and I had never done anything like this in my life! In my eagerness to serve, I had failed to stop and consider what I was reasonably able to do. I didn't factor in that I had a galley kitchen, was raising five children (three of whom I was homeschooling), and was pregnant with baby number six. "What do you want me to do, God?" I considered calling the bride and confessing that I wasn't going to be able to take on this task, after all . . . then rejected this idea. Somehow I just knew God was going to help me bless this couple.

And sure enough, a true miracle took place: God poured out his Divine Mercy upon me, making up for my personal shortcomings during my brief career as a free wedding cake baker and decorator. What I lacked in baking skills, I made up for in networking. By calling other Catholic women, telling them about this sweet young couple, and asking for their help, I found three women willing to bake cakes. My mother found six round cake pans at a garage sale, and I felt that Mother Mary was smiling down on me, coaxing me along.

Now I needed to find a cake decorator. It is one thing to bake a cake, but it is another to decorate it for a wedding! Thankfully, God once again made up for my shortcomings and "filled in the cracks." Two weeks before the wedding, I was waiting at my son's survival/nature class when another mother arrived and started to tell me about the wedding cake she had just made for one of her relatives. She pulled out her phone and showed me pictures of her gorgeously decorated cakes. She and I spent the whole day before the wedding decorating the cakes—the project was finished!

The following night as I was leaving the reception, ready to retire my wedding cake apron forever, one of the kitchen staff members stopped me. She asked, "Are *you* the cake lady? We heard you volunteered to bake these. I have to tell you that the catering staff and I agree: we have never had such fresh and delicious cake."

I was shocked, but after thinking about it, I had to agree with her. Those cakes were delicious and beautifully decorated. Even more, though, they were a gift of the whole Christian community of women who stepped forward to help this young bride.

This experience taught me a lesson about the importance of receiving the Divine Mercy of Christ, and how that mercy multiplies as we live it out and extend it to others. As I pondered the whole chain of events, I could see that Christ honored my good intention to do a merciful deed by providing help every step of the way, multiplying my gift of mercy through the talents of others around me to provide a far superior gift than any I could have given on my own.

When we offer mercy to others, we become Christ's hands and feet in the world; in responding to his command to love our neighbor as we love him we will find the gospel peace he wants to give us.

## Respond to God's Call in Deed, Word, and Prayer

*Deed*: Give a spontaneous gift to an unsuspecting person today. It doesn't have to be a big gift. Bake some extra cookies; bring a friend lunch or even a cup of tea or coffee. You can even give the gift of yourself: babysit for a friend, offer a carpool ride, or make a surprise visit.

*Word*: Take a few minutes to write down a list of the blessings you have been given in your life. Thank God for these gifts.

*Prayer*: As you discern God's will for how you are to live mercifully, take a moment to pray the following prayer from the *Diary* of St. Faustina on accepting the will of God:

> O my God, I am ready to accept Your will in every detail, whatever it may be. However You may direct me, I will bless You. Whatever You ask of me I will do with the help of Your grace. Whatever Your holy will regarding me might be, I accept it with my whole heart and soul. (1356)

# CHAPTER 4

# The Corporal Works of *Mercy*

I understand souls who are suffering against hope, for I have gone through that fire myself. But God will not give [us anything] beyond our strength. (386)

The other day I (Michele) took my nine-month-old for a routine checkup at the Nationwide Children's Hospital. As we walked down the blue painted line of the hallway, my son Jacob announced, "Mom, I hate this place. I hope I never have to go here again!"

I understood just what he meant. Memories of the thirty-five days and nights we had spent here with him were still fresh and a little painful. Yet Jacob's medical crisis taught me firsthand—as nothing else could have—about the merciful heart of Christ, and how

Divine Mercy touches the lives of those who need it most. Squeezing my son's hand, I breathed a prayer of thanks as my thoughts turned back to the darkness that had descended upon our family just a few years before.

I had just completed a group study on Marian Consecration on the Feast of the Immaculate Conception, December 8, 2011—a Thursday. The very next day Jacob started to complain of a stomachache and of not feeling quite right. As a nurse, I attributed these symptoms to a virus.

That Sunday morning, he fell in the parking lot on the way into Mass. We were running late so we hurried him to his feet, but I had a bad feeling in my gut, that intuitive "mom feeling" we all get from time to time. Over the next few days Jacob's condition worsened. When he became too weak to walk on his own, we were finally admitted to Children's Hospital for a CAT scan and a spinal tap. The spinal tap showed elevated levels of a protein that indicates Guillain-Barré syndrome, a rare autoimmune disease that causes your own antibodies to attack the nervous system. Jacob's brain could no longer send any messages to his muscles. And while he was expected to fully recover, it was expected to take a year—and his condition would get worse before it got any better. So we moved up to the neurology unit with Jacob and stayed with him as he became completely paralyzed from the chest down.

We spent the next thirty-five days at the hospital. I was there during the day, and my husband did the night shift. With intensive therapy, the downward trend reversed and Jacob slowly recovered day by day. In the weeks that followed, Jesus sustained us with his peace (surely a grace received through all the prayers being offered for us) as our friends and relatives met our physical needs.

We were the beneficiaries of countless corporal and spiritual works of mercy; I will never forget all the family and friends who visited, brought gifts and often three meals a day, and prayed day and night for our son. Priests stopped by to anoint Jacob and bring us Communion. Friends of friends whom we didn't know reached out to us because they heard our story and wanted to help. They visited or sent gift cards, prayers, and well wishes.

All across the country, people prayed for us. I could feel the strength from those prayers every day as Masses were offered for Jacob's healing. And God answered those prayers. People began to call Jacob "the miracle boy": by his six-week follow up, he was completely normal, months ahead of schedule. Seeing him walk around, you would never have known he had been in a wheelchair just a few weeks before.

The whole experience taught us a great deal about mercy because we were the recipients of so much of it. Over and over I experienced the truth of the words traditionally attributed to St. Teresa of Ávila:

Christ has no body now on earth but yours;
    no hands but yours; no feet but yours.
Yours are the eyes through which the compassion
    of Christ must look out on the world.
Yours are the feet with which he is to go about
    doing good.
Yours are the hands with which he is to bless his
    people.

Through this shower of mercy on my family, I learned how to treat others when they are in a difficult situation and what it means to receive Divine Mercy and pass it on to others.

## What Are the Corporal Works of Mercy?

In her *Diary*, St. Faustina recalls encountering Christ through an act of service (also known as a work of mercy) as she worked at the door of the convent.

> Jesus came to the main entrance today, under the guise of a poor young man. This young man, emaciated, barefoot and bareheaded, and with his clothes in tatters, was frozen because the day was cold and rainy. He asked for something hot to eat. So I went to the kitchen, but found nothing there for the poor. But, after searching around for some time, I succeeded in finding some soup, which I reheated and into which I crumbled some bread, and I gave it to the poor young man, who ate it. As I was taking the bowl from him, he gave me to know that He was the Lord of heaven and earth. When I saw Him as He was, He vanished from my sight. (1312)

We may not get to physically see Jesus, but we can serve Christ in our everyday lives through our service to our families and to others. Each work of mercy is a natural expression of the Divine Mercy poured out in our lives, especially when we offer these acts with the intention of allowing his mercy to pass through our heart and souls to our neighbors.[1]

There are fourteen works of mercy in all: seven corporal, based on bodily needs; and seven spiritual, which attend to the needs of the soul. The ancient roots of corporal works of mercy can be traced to the Gospel of Matthew,

> Then the king will say to those on his right, "Come, you who are blessed by my Father. Inherit the kingdom prepared for you from the foundation of the world. For I was hungry and you gave me food, I was thirsty and you gave me drink, a stranger and you welcomed me, naked and you clothed me, ill and you cared for me, in prison and you visited me." Then the righteous will answer him and say, "Lord, when did we see you hungry and feed you, or thirsty and give you drink? When did we see you a stranger and welcome you, or naked and clothe you? When did we see you ill or in prison, and visit you?" And the king will say to them in reply, "Amen, I say to you, whatever you did for one of these least brothers of mine, you did for me." (Mt 25:34–40)

The seven corporal works of mercy are:

1. Feed the hungry.
2. Give drink to the thirsty.
3. Clothe the naked.
4. Shelter the homeless.
5. Visit the sick.
6. Visit the imprisoned.
7. Bury the dead. (see Tb 1:17–18)

We'll talk about the spiritual works of mercy in the next chapter. As mothers, we must embody these works of mercy not just for our children but for all those around us—including strangers, as God gives us opportunities. Since this is the more "practical" section of the book we would like to share some ways we as moms have learned to live out these works of mercy in our daily lives. We've also included some ideas from our friends who have led us by their example.

Don't worry, you don't have to start your own soup kitchen or visit a developing country. God will provide little opportunities every day through your interactions with others, whether you are driving in your car, reading through your e-mail, or even interacting on Facebook. Every morning, ask God to give you wisdom and resolve, and pray that you are able to discern easily what he is calling you to do. Ask Jesus to allow you to be his hands and feet on earth as an instrument of mercy.

With each work of mercy we have included a quotation from the *Diary*. As you read, ponder these short quotations and consider how God is asking you to spread Divine Mercy.

### Feed the Hungry

> Today I imprudently asked two poor children if they really had nothing to eat at home. The children, without answering me, walked away from the gate. I understood how difficult it was for them to speak about their poverty, so I went after them in a hurry and brought them back, giving them as much as I had permission for. (1297)

*Feed your family with love and prayer.* As mothers, we are always feeding the hungry. Our children are always "starving." At times life seems like a constant cycle of preparing meals, packing lunches, and fixing snacks. Just when we get everything all cleaned up, it's time to start over again! We can turn this mundane task into an act of mercy when we deliberately do the cooking with love and prayer.[2] As you pack each lunch box, pray specifically for that child. Pray the Chaplet of Divine Mercy for your family while you are making dinner.

Even though I spend much of my day in the kitchen, when I remember to pray through those times I can turn them into moments of mercy. Each time I pray over my stove, I am feeding not only stomachs, but souls. Take time this week to make something special for your family and pray for them as you prepare it. As you prepare food for your family, be sure to remember to the Lord those who go without food.

*Prepare and deliver a meal.* When friends and extended family members—including parish family—are going through a tough time, receiving a hot meal can be a much-needed source of encouragement. Websites such as mealtrain.com and carecalendar.org offer free meal calendar services, making it very easy to coordinate through e-mail to assist new mothers or those who are facing other challenges such as an illness or financial difficulties.

*Send a gift card if you can't cook for others.* If bringing a meal is too difficult with your family schedule, sending gift cards to local restaurants is a simple way to give a family a hot meal. Another way to help a family going through a hard time is to pay for school lunches if they have children in school. This takes one thing off the mother's plate when she is juggling more than she can handle.

*Make a sacrifice and donate the money to the poor.* In today's world, hunger is a very real and serious problem. Every four seconds a child dies from hunger![3] Our parish partners with Hands Together, an organization that helps the poor in Haiti (www.handstogether.org). The priest who runs the program told us about Haitian children who are so hungry that their mothers mix dirt with spices and bake the mixture in the sun so the children have something to eat. The dirt is full of parasites and mixed with sewage. Can you imagine having to feed that to your children?

One practice our family has adopted is making a sacrifice of some type, such as giving up sweets. We take the money saved on not buying junk food and give it to our parish collection for the children of Haiti. If you are wondering how to help, one organization Emily and I have partnered with is Mary's Meals International. They believe that every child deserves an education and enough to eat. By using an army of volunteers they can stretch a dollar far and provide meals for a student for an entire year for less than twenty dollars! If you would like to know more, contact Mary's Meals International (www.marysmealsusa.org/en/).

Lent and Advent are especially good times to encourage your family to make sacrifices and set money aside for the poor. Fr. Michael Gaitley recommends doing this all year long and collecting the money in a "Mercy Fund" to use for helping others.[4] Emily and I have a friend who follows this practice; she calls the jar she collects the money in her Sunshine

Jar because her family uses the funds to bring a little sunshine into someone else's life.

*Share a lunch.* Many schools have a subsidized lunch program. In 2013 over thirty-one million students received over five billion free or reduced-cost lunches.[5] When school is closed, some children have a hard time getting nutritious food. One simple way to help is to donate nonperishable lunches to a local school or food pantry to be given out to those students.

### Give Drink to the Thirsty

> Once, when I returned to my cell, I was so tired that I had to rest a moment before I started to undress, and when I was already undressed, one of the sisters asked me to fetch her some hot water. Although I was tired, I dressed quickly and brought her the water she wanted, even though it was quite a long walk from the cell to the kitchen, and the mud was ankle-deep. When I re-entered my cell, I saw the ciborium with the Blessed Sacrament, and I heard this voice, **Take this ciborium and bring it to the tabernacle.** I hesitated at first, but when I approached and touched it, I heard these words, **Approach each of the sisters with the same love with which you approach Me; and whatever you do for them, you do it for Me.** A moment later, I saw that I was alone. (285)

Approach your family as you would approach Christ. It happens to me every morning. After I prepare breakfast for my kids and finally sit down to eat my nice hot meal someone asks, "Can I have some more water?"

And every day I think, "Seriously, I just sat down. Can't you get it for yourself?" But I get up and begrudgingly serve a cup of water, usually with a side of eye rolling and annoyed sighing. But if Jesus were sitting at my table, would I treat him like that? Of course not!

So I try to serve my family with patience and kindness. It can be very difficult always to be kind when living in close proximity with other people. Yet these small sacrifices quench not only their physical thirst but their spiritual thirst for love.

*Donate drinks to an after-school program or clean water program.* Each time we get up at a meal or in the middle of the night to fetch a cup of water for someone we love, we are given another opportunity to remember those who struggle to find clean water for themselves and their families. While we are blessed to have fresh water all the time, it is not that way for everyone in the world: nearly 750,000 people lack access to a supply of safe water and more than 840,000 people die each year from water-related diseases.[6] Every minute a child somewhere in the world dies of a water-related disease.[7] Last year, as I was praying about what our family Lenten sacrifice should be, I slipped on a piece of paper that turned out to be my daughter's art project, a large poster that read "Give Drink to the Thirsty" and had pictures of children giving others drinks. As part of the school's theme for the year, she had listed several ways she could quench the thirst of her neighbor. One simple thing she and her classmates were able to do was to collect drinks for an after-school program for underprivileged children.

Another simple way we can help is by making a donation to a clean water project such as Catholic Relief Services provides in some developing countries (www.crs.org/water-sanitation).

*Hand out water.* When the heat soars in the summertime, keep small bottles of water in your car or purse to pass out to people you see on the street. Tape an inspiring quotation or prayer or other small message of encouragement to the bottle. Consider including the name and address of a nearby food pantry or soup kitchen on the label as well.

### Clothe the Naked

Where there is genuine virtue, there must be sacrifice as well; one's whole life must be a sacrifice. It is only by means of sacrifice that souls can become useful. It is my self-sacrifice which, in my relationship with my neighbor, can give glory to God, but God's love must flow through this sacrifice, because everything is concentrated in this love and takes its value from it. (1358)

How many coats do you have hanging in your hall closet right now? The other day I looked in our hallway closet and counted forty-two coats for six people! Then I thought of that verse in Scripture where Jesus says, "Whoever has two tunics should share with the person who has none" (Lk 3:11).

I know we need different coats for different seasons and even different outfits . . . but *forty-two coats?!*

*Donate excess or outgrown clothing.* For me, shopping can be a real stress reducer; nothing makes me feel better than finding a good deal. Every closet in my home is overstuffed, with extra clothes in the basement. It's really easy for me to become a hoarder. And so, my efforts to live out the gospel call to mercy benefit receiver and giver alike. Each time I bring an armful to St. Vincent de Paul, my surplus blesses another family—and I get to grow in detachment! There are many Catholic organizations like Birthright that will sell your gently used clothing at thrift stores and use the money to help those in need.

*Make a sacrifice and donate the money you save.* Another way to grow in generosity is to learn to live more simply, making do or seeking out second-hand solutions rather than running to the store to buy what you need. You can then donate the money you save through this sacrifice to an organization that provides clothing to those who need it. This is why I began this section with the quotation about sacrifice from Faustina's *Diary.* The Lord values our giving more when we make a sacrifice to accomplish it as did the widow with her mite (Mk 12:41–44). Jesus said she gave more than anyone because she gave from her poverty, not from her wealth.

*Sponsor a child.* I will never forget the poverty I encountered one summer at a Jamaican orphanage for abandoned children with disabilities run by Mustard Seed Communities (www.mustardseed.com). We spent most of the mission trip feeding the children and playing with them.

I noticed all the little children in the AIDS home were running around wearing just diapers, and very full ones at that. I asked the staff if I could help change diapers, thinking they were too busy to keep up with the job. They replied that because of the high cost of diapers, they only changed the diapers when they absolutely had to, since all of the funding went to buying medications to treat HIV. Sadly, there was not even enough money to treat all the children, so only the sickest received medicine.

That memory stuck with me. At the time I was a very new mother (just eight weeks pregnant with my first) and couldn't imagine having to choose between clothes and medicine for my children. Yet when I saw those sick children, I recognized true poverty, and more than anything I wanted to help. Would you? You can help clothe the naked by sponsoring a child through a Catholic nonprofit organization called Unbound, formerly known as Christian Foundation for Children and Aging (www.unbound.org). Both Unbound and Mustard Seed Communities work with children in developing countries and allow you to pick a specific child in whose life you can help make a difference for a small monthly donation.

### Shelter the Homeless

> This morning, five unemployed men came to the gate and insisted on being let in. When Sister N. had argued with them for quite a while and could not make them go away, she then came to the chapel to find Mother [Irene], who told me to go. When I was still a good way from the gate I could hear them banging loudly. At first, I was overcome with doubt and fear, and I did not know whether to open the gate or, like Sister N., to answer them

through the little window. But suddenly I heard a voice in my soul saying, **Go and open the gate and talk to them as sweetly as you talk to Me.**

I opened the gate at once and approached the most menacing of them and began to speak to them with such sweetness and calm that they did not know what to do with themselves. And they too began to speak gently. (1377)

My son had to memorize the corporal and spiritual works of mercy one year. When we got to this one, no matter how many times I corrected him, he always recited, "Home the homeless."

*Open your home to those who need spiritual shelter.* While providing shelter for your family is a necessity, making it a *home* where their faith is learned and shared is a mercy. If we live out our faith, our homes can be spiritual shelters to those who come into them and learn about God. So many people today don't teach their children about God or share their faith with others. Once our children had some new friends over, and we prayed grace before lunch. The friends were intrigued and asked what we were doing. I explained what prayer was and a little bit about some of the religious art in our home.

One little boy replied, "My mom said there is no such thing as God or the devil!" That was so sad to me, yet we can always plant little seeds of faith and hope in those who enter our homes. Several moms have shared with me how they have been a shelter to one of their children's friends, especially during the teenage years, and influenced their faith. By being inviting of our children's friends into our homes full of love and sharing our faith in small ways, we can have a big impact.

*Reach out right through your car window.* Another way to reach out to the homeless is right through your car window. Yes, it can be hard to know what to do when you see homeless people. Their unkempt appearance, smell, or strange demeanor can be unsettling. On the other hand, if God wants you to reach out to help, be brave. You never know what blessing you might be passing up if you just roll up the window and keep on driving.

The other day as she was sitting at a red light, Emily noticed a beautiful twenty-year-old standing a few feet away with a sign that read, "Help Me, I am Homeless." Emily couldn't get her out of her mind; she decided to pick up a fast food dinner for the young woman. Returning to the intersection, Emily got out of her car and went over to the young woman to hand her the meal and sat with her a few moments while she ate. As the young woman shared her story, it was evident that her suffering had begun long before she became homeless. It began years ago, when her family broke apart leaving her feeling fragmented and abandoned.

Emily offered the young woman the number for our local Catholic Social Services, which had a program that could help her. The girl agreed to call. Emily asked her, "Do you believe in Jesus?"

"I want to, but it is hard, you know?"

Emily hugged her and told her about St. Faustina, a young woman who knew all about suffering. The homeless girl listened intently. Emily was the first person who had stopped and talked to her, who cared enough to tell her of a God who is merciful . . . and a saint who suffered, just as she was suffering.

*Be intentional with your presence.* If you're a bit more introverted like me, you can keep in your car small baggies filled with nonperishable food items like granola bars and packaged snacks; you can tuck prayer cards into the baggies and hand them to the homeless person with a smile and a "God bless you." Taking just a moment to acknowledge the presence of the person—to look them in the eye as you give them a small token—is a true gift and an important reminder to both of you of the human dignity of each person.

*Support local organizations that help the poor get back on their feet.* Check your parish bulletin for opportunities to volunteer at a shelter or soup kitchen, or to support other groups such as Habitat for Humanity or St. Vincent de Paul. Donate toiletries or other items to a local crisis pregnancy center or domestic violence shelter.

"Adopt" a local shelter and do what you can to spread the word about its presence as well as its needs in your parish bulletin and in your community.

### Visit the Sick

> I went in and rendered a service to a seriously sick person. When I returned to my room, I suddenly saw the Lord Jesus, who said, **My daughter, you gave Me greater pleasure by rendering Me that service than if you had prayed for a long time.** I answered, "But it was not to You, Jesus, but to that patient that I rendered this service." And the Lord

answered me, **"Yes, My daughter, but whatever you for your neighbor, you do for Me."** (1029)

A recent study from the University of Michigan reported a dramatic decline in empathy over the past thirty years, with the sharpest decline in the past ten years. The researchers also reported that narcissism is at an all-time high.[8]

*Teach your children to tend the sick at home.* Whenever someone is sick in our home, I use it as a time to teach empathy. Everyone caters to the person who is sick. The sick family member gets to choose what is on TV and what we eat. Everyone helps with the sick person's chores—even though "it's not fair." We remind the children that loving someone means being willing to make sacrifices. Helping a sick sibling or parent helps them to grow in mercy, so they get in the habit of sharing that mercy with others.

*Tend the sick outside your home.* Similarly, it's important to tend to the sick outside your own home. Taking children to visit very sick people can be daunting. And yet, when my son was in the hospital for over a month, I learned the irreplaceable value of visiting the sick. Jacob's second-grade classmates and their parents became my "mercy superstars." His classmates came up to the hospital to play with him during his recovery, bringing things that could occupy him, like board games, remote-control helicopters, videos, and snacks. He could not walk, and yet his friends came and played wheelchair basketball with him and even sent a small portable hoop to his room so he could shoot from his bed.

I learned a lot from those kids, and the company of their parents was so reassuring. Many shared their trials in life and how they survived. One had had a child go through cancer; another came for a visit with pizza after a checkup with her daughter in the clinic just a few floors down in the hospital. These moms understood the importance of spending time with someone who is sick! Now if I know of someone who is in the hospital, I try my hardest to make a visit.

*Send a card and gift of prayer.* If I can't visit, I send a Mass card for their healing to the person who is ill and promise my prayers. I also use an app on my phone called Echo Prayer Manager (new.echoprayer.com) to remind me to pray for them every day while they are recovering. While Jacob's room was covered in cards, I know from working in hospitals and nursing homes for years that many patients in rooms with bare walls feel forgotten. This small gesture can really brighten someone's day.

*Give a "merciful ride."* When Jacob was sick and when I had new babies, I needed help getting my other kids to school and events. One way to help out mothers who are housebound due to illness or the exhaustion of new motherhood is by offering a "merciful ride." Extending a drop-off or pickup, without expecting the favor to be returned, can be a real lifesaver to moms.

## Visit the Imprisoned

> O my Jesus, when shall we look upon souls with higher motives in mind? When will our judgments be true? You give us occasions to practice deeds of mercy, and instead we use the occasions to pass judgment. (1269)

Although prison ministry is a very important and much-needed ministry in our Church, taking a field trip to the local correctional institution with your children probably isn't on the list of prudent things to do. So how can we live out this particular work of mercy?

*Support prison ministries.* A few years ago my friend Kim called and asked if I could bake cookies for a ministry called Kairos Prison Ministry. She was going on retreat with forty-two female inmates to help them build Christian community within the correctional facility—and she needed to bring over seven hundred cookies as refreshments. All I had to do was make homemade chocolate chip cookies and pray for the inmates while I baked. This was a great opportunity to bring my children into the project because they love to be in the kitchen with me and help cook, especially when there would certainly be a few extra chocolate chip cookies left over!

As we baked I shared what the cookies were for and we prayed together for those who would receive the cookies. After the retreat Kim sent me this message: "I can't tell you how much the women appreciated the cookies. They were moved to tears to think that people care about them. There were many women on the retreat who were in for murder or other offenses that keep them in jail for so long. No one visits or writes them, and definitely no one makes them cookies. They were overwhelmed with love." This was such a simple task, and I didn't even have to leave my kitchen! Kim came over and picked up the cookies to take to the retreat. I have seen parishes do collections for Kairos Prison Ministry and collect the cookies right in the vestibule of the church to make it easy for people to participate. If you would like to get something started at your parish, go to kpmifoundation.org.

*Pray for priests.* While it isn't always possible for us to visit the imprisoned in person, we can support the priests who say Mass in prisons. They often work with limited supplies for their ministry. If you are crafty, you can make altar cloths to donate for priests to take to the prisons or nursing homes. It makes for a great first-time sewing project for yourself and to teach your children.

*Visit a nursing home.* Another way to live out this work of mercy is to help those who are imprisoned in other ways, such as those who live in memory care facilities or are isolated in nursing homes and cannot leave. We have had several family members who have lived in nursing homes, and we always try to make it a priority on Sunday to visit them. When we are there, we encourage our children to show off their talents to all the residents gathered in the common area. While my kids were very little, this meant turning lopsided somersaults and singing cute songs. Now that they are older, they play the piano and perform choreographed dances as the residents smile, sing along, and laugh with them.

As mothers we can also be good examples to others and to our children by celebrating special events with works of mercy. We were recently invited to a birthday party just before Christmas. The host served the guests a meal in her home and then everyone headed out Christmas caroling at a local nursing home.

*Befriend a shut-in.* Shut-ins are also those who may be imprisoned in their own homes. When I was young my parents had a small Rosary group at our parish, and every week we picked up an elderly gentleman to pray with us. As he was unable to drive anywhere himself, this weekly Sunday trip was very important to him. We not only gave him a ride, we invited him to be a part of our crazy family of ten and take part in our conversation and our life.

When my friend and I led a study group on Divine Mercy (*Consoling the Heart of Jesus*, by Fr. Michael Gaitley), a woman with terminal cancer saw the announcement in our parish bulletin and decided to join us. She was very lonely and had been alienated from the Church for a long time. Yet we welcomed her, and she returned to the Catholic faith and found peace through this study. Since her only daughter lived far away, we journeyed with her as her health deteriorated, running errands for her and taking her to church.

As the cancer progressed, we spent time with her in hospice. She liked to paint watercolor images and gave some to my children when we visited. They still remember visiting an "artist" at the hospital. At the end of her life, she was able to receive the Anointing of the Sick, and some of my friends were at her bedside at the hour of her death, praying the Chaplet of Divine Mercy. We buried her on my birthday, and I remember thinking that being able to be with her during those last few months was the best gift I had received that year.

*Be a compassionate listener.* My aunt knew a woman (we'll call her "Annie") who struggled with sobriety; Annie kept "falling" in her addiction, but also kept trying to get to daily Mass and get back to God. At one point my aunt reached out to Annie, as did some of the women who prayed the Rosary after daily Mass, which Annie often joined. They listened to her story: how she had lived with several children in a homeless shelter, been caught in an abusive relationship, and struggled with the physical, emotional, mental, and spiritual consequences of alcoholism. Imprisoned in the guilt and shame of her addiction, Annie was once again living in a homeless shelter, trying to get help. Compassionate listening to someone who is "imprisoned" by addiction is, indeed, a work of mercy.

### Bury the Dead

> For my homeland is in heaven—this I firmly believe. (1589)

I remember driving to a wake with my parents and complaining to my mom, "Why do we have to go to this wake? I didn't even know the person!" My mom explained that we didn't go for the person who had died, but to comfort their family members and express our sorrow for their loss.

How can we "bury the dead" in the literal sense? One important way is to advocate "in word, deed, and prayer" for the proper funeral for and burial of deceased family members—including the appropriate disposition of ashes, in the case of cremation. The benefits of this particular work of mercy extend to both the living and the dead; by helping the bereaved to mourn, we are given an opportunity to deal with death physically, spiritually, and emotionally—and to teach our children as well. What are some other ways we can teach our children to practice this work of mercy?

*Attend wakes, funerals, and burials.* Attending a wake, funeral, and burial can be a very touching act of mercy. I try to attend wakes and funerals as much as my schedule allows, and if my children are with me, I take them along. This helps the children come to see death as a part of life and encourages them to live with heaven in their minds and hearts. The presence of babies and well-mannered young children can also be a comfort to the bereaved.

*Send a Mass card or have a Mass offered.* When attending the wake or funeral isn't possible, send the gift of a Mass card to the family as a way of living mercy without actually leaving your house. Check with your parish office about having a Mass offered in memory of the deceased. Alternatively, many religious orders have cards they will send you. I keep a small stack of them in a greeting card organizer. When I need a card, I am able to pick out a beautiful card decorated with Catholic art and send it to a grieving friend. At the same time I fill out a form to send to the religious order so they know who to pray for (consider offering a modest stipend to support their work). I can then tuck both envelopes in my mailbox, put the flag up and voilà! Mercy in the mail. If you don't want to walk to the mailbox, visit the Marians of the Immaculate Conception's site and order online, they will mail it for you!

In the next chapter, Emily reflects on the spiritual works of mercy. As you continue to read, it is our sincere hope that you will not feel overwhelmed at the prospect of adding more items to your "to-do" list. Rather, we pray that you will come to see these opportunities that arise as moments for you to draw upon the deep ocean of God's mercy and share it with the world. It's not about draining your own limited resources, but about tapping into the heart of Christ. In the words of Pope Francis, "This is the opportune moment to change our lives!"[9]

Start with one act of mercy each day and ask the great Apostle of Divine Mercy, St. Faustina, to "obtain for us the grace of living and walking always according to the mercy of God."[10]

### Respond to God's Call in Deed, Word, and Prayer

*Deed*: Make a list of at least three ways you feel called to live out the corporal works of mercy in your life. Select ideas from the book or come up with your own. Try to do at least one small thing each day this week. Share your experiences with us at divinemercyformoms.com.

*Word*: Order Mass cards or Catholic stationery to have handy when you need to write to someone who could use prayers or a word of encouragement. Good places to buy these cards include the Marians of the Immaculate Conception and the Franciscan Friars, T.O.R.[11] Stationery is available at catholicstationery.com or pioprints.com.

*Prayer*: Start a prayer journal or download a prayer app like Echo Prayer Manager that will help you keep track of prayer intentions.

# CHAPTER 5

# The Spiritual Works of *Mercy*

**Write this for the many souls who are often worried because they do not have the material means with which to carry out an act of mercy. Yet spiritual mercy, which requires neither permissions nor storehouses, is much more meritorious and is within the grasp of every soul. If a soul does not exercise mercy somehow or other, it will not obtain My mercy on the day of judgment. Oh, if only souls knew how to gather eternal treasure for themselves, they would not be judged, for they would forestall My judgment with their mercy.** (1317)

The idea of comforting or ministering to others might seem a bit overwhelming to those of us who are caught up in the details of running our households. I know I

(Emily) sometimes feel as though I am already juggling too many balls. How in the world can I do one more thing?

The spiritual works of mercy remind us to consider the person behind the "work," a person who needs our love, care, and compassion no matter who they are or how our paths cross. Our goal is to embody the mercy of Christ by reaching out and showing others compassion as the opportunities arise. The following are the spiritual works of mercy:

1. Counsel the doubtful.

2. Instruct the ignorant.

3. Admonish sinners.

4. Comfort the afflicted.

5. Forgive offenses.

6. Bear wrongs patiently.

7. Pray for the living and the dead.

In the school parking lot, sitting on the third baseline, and standing in line at the grocery store checkout, I have had occasions to speak to others about God and to practice the spiritual works of mercy outlined in *The Catechism of the Catholic Church*: to "come to the aid of our neighbor in his spiritual and bodily necessities. Instructing, advising, consoling, comforting are spiritual works of mercy, as are forgiving and bearing wrongs patiently" (CCC 2447).

Many times, chances to practice mercy arise as we witness the sufferings of others, or are reminded of the compassionate heart of Jesus in our own times of distress. Suffering pinpricks the heart to wake up and notice what really matters. For Catholics, the journey to holiness is not a solitary expedition in which we remain engrossed in our own interior lives. Rather we must be inspired to reach out into our communities to bring others closer to Christ. In the words of St. Mother Teresa of Calcutta:

> The greatest disease in the West today is not TB or leprosy; it is being unwanted, unloved, and uncared for. We can cure physical diseases with medicine, but the only cure for loneliness, despair, and hopelessness is love. There are many in the world who are dying for a piece of bread but there are many more dying for a little love. The poverty in the West is a different kind of poverty—it is not only a poverty of loneliness but also of spirituality. There's a hunger for love, as there is a hunger for God.[1]

## Sharing Mercy through Motherhood

Motherhood is an amazing opportunity to expand our world, bring love to others, and help break the cycle of loneliness. Our relationships with other parents can encompass more than shared experiences, like sports teams and activities; the universal nature of motherhood allows us to build bridges to be able to speak about our Faith and to serve others as Christ would.

As women, we find it easy to stay in the world of materialism (both our concern for our material possessions and affairs and the increasingly prevalent belief in our society that only material things—the things that we can see, feel, and measure—exist) and keep to safe topics of conversation. It is hard to break out of this type of conversation and run the risk of offending someone or sounding like a religious fanatic, especially when others just don't live outside of this "safe zone." But our Faith and our Church call us to be bold. In 2013, at World Youth Day in Rio de Janeiro, Pope Francis summarized his desire to proclaim the Gospel and reach out to others: "I want the Church to go out onto the streets! . . . The parishes, the schools, the institutions are made for going out!"[2]

We cannot just wait for others to come to us; we must join this mission to go out to into the world to seek souls. This journey is one in which we become willing to be the hands and feet of Christ to go out to others and not only share with them the Good News but show them through our actions that God loves them. This requires that we give of ourselves.

Our job is to respond to suffering with compassion and love. The training we receive in motherhood, in caring for our own children, equips us to extend that love to others. Motherhood stretches your heart—once you have loved a child, your ability to love is permanently expanded.

In her teaching, the Church constantly returns to the relationship between charity and justice: "When we attend to the needs of those in want, we give them what is theirs, not ours. More than performing works of mercy, we are paying a debt of justice" (*CCC* 2446, quoting St. Gregory the Great).

When we practice works of mercy we bring dignity to others and store up eternal treasure for ourselves. Let's take a closer look at each of the spiritual works of mercy now.

## Counsel the Doubtful

> Today a girl came to see me. I saw that she was
> suffering, but not so much in body as in soul. I
> comforted her as much as I could, but my words
> of consolation were not enough. She was a poor
> orphan with a soul plunged in bitterness and pain.
> She opened her soul to me and told me everything.
> I understood that, in this case, simple words of
> consolation would not be enough. I fervently inter-
> ceded with the Lord for that soul and offered Him
> my joy so that He would give it to her and take all
> feeling of joy away from me. And the Lord heard
> my prayer. I was left only with the consolation that
> she had been consoled. (864)

Many of our youth seem to be plagued with bitterness
and pain and to be questioning the existence of God.
Just listen to the popular music on the radio that tells
a story of distrust, pain, loss, and lust. This quotation
from St. Faustina's *Diary* brings up the direct reality
that Christ is asking us to bring hope and joy to those
caught in this confusion. As Catholics, we are not to
run from others but to be an anchor of support during
their difficult times. When we provide counsel to others it is based on relationship, which includes offering
empathy, listening to the details of the situation, and
weighing in when asked. Counseling the doubtful
requires us to slow down so that we can see others
in spiritual need, and we are to lead as much by our
example as by our words. As a friend recently pointed
out to us, "Just simple faith is what makes all instruction meaningful. Instruction should be an invitation—
let God do the rest."

*Don't worry, be happy:* As women, we can easily turn to doubt and worry. These doubts begin with just a thought but when we allow it to fester, we can lose our ability to trust God and his plan for us. The Lord asks us not to worry about the future, but rather to have faith. In Matthew 6:26, Jesus tells us, "Look at the birds in the sky; they do not sow or reap, they gather nothing into barns, yet your heavenly Father feeds them. Are you not more important than they?" When you feel yourself heading down the dark road of doubting, reach out to others for counsel, support, and spiritual direction. Our worries are never productive; they just cloud up our thinking.

*Encourage the overwhelmed.* A friend and I were both picking up our children from a preschool class when her two-year-old had a meltdown in the church parking lot. She looked stressed and exhausted as she tried to get him into the car. When I went over to give her a hand, she said to me, "Motherhood is a like a concentration camp—you just move stones from one pile to the next." Overwhelmed by her state in life, she needed someone to help her in that moment.

Smiling sympathetically, I reminded her of something the Little Flower, St. Thérèse, said: "One small act done with love is powerful!" We will never be perfect in following God's will, but if we are willing to serve him through the mundane and ordinary tasks of life we will bring glory to God.

St. Faustina reinforces this idea: "Pure love is capable of great deeds, and it is not broken by difficulty or adversity. As it remains strong in the midst of great difficulties, so too it perseveres in the toilsome and drab life of each day. It knows that only one thing is needed to please God: to do even the smallest things out of great love" (140). These two incredible saints share a powerful insight: what we do has meaning whether we attach meaning to it or not.

*Invite people back to the Catholic Church.* I can't tell you how many times I have heard the words "I grew up Catholic." Many people have lost their faith through doubts that were never addressed or due to wounds that were never healed; they need that "counsel" piece to bring them home. When we are willing to listen, pray, and respond we can help others in their spiritual journey. By inviting people back to the Faith we encourage them to take a second look at the Church. Sometimes it is uncomfortable to engage in these types of conversations, but if you plant the seeds, God will water them.

### Instruct the Ignorant

> We come to be educated—like a small child, our soul has constant need of education. (377)

Everyone longs for the truth that can only be found in Christ. In John 18:38, Pontius Pilate poses the question, "What is truth?" We have a great privilege to make the truths of the Faith presentable and attractive to others. In the words of Pope Francis, "The truth is not grasped as a thing; the truth is encountered. It is not a possession; it is an encounter with a Person."[3]

We are called to be witnesses, to proclaim God's love to others and to instruct them in the ways of Christ. When we instruct others with love and compassion, the natural beauty and authenticity of the Catholic Faith will entice them to take a closer look. This is true with our neighbors, our friends, and even our children!

*Lead with charity.* Whenever we instruct the ignorant, we must remember to do so with complete charity as we humbly attempt to lead others to Christ. This is especially true regarding our children. In an age of infinite choices, it is important that we model authentic love in order to help our children choose the Catholic faith.

*Cultivate "good soil" for your children.* Seek out learning environments that are supportive of your children's faith. Be aware of outside influences on their moral development: friends, music and entertainment, and other pastimes. Invest in Catholic summer camp or Vacation Bible School; these are a great ways to enrich your children's faith formation that complement what they are learning during the school year. Children thrive when what we teach them at home is reinforced in a fun environment.

*Find good role models.* Seek out mentors outside your family, such as youth ministers, teachers, and coaches, to influence your children and reinforce the values you are teaching at home. Keep the lines of communication open, especially as your children reach their teen years, and encourage them to connect with others who are mature in their faith.

*Use car time to build up your children's faith life.* I try to play Catholic radio for a few minutes when the kids are in the car before switching it to their favorite station. If you don't have Catholic radio in your area you can stream it live on your smart phone (try www.stgabrielradio.com). Car time is also a great time to figure out what is going on with your children, who their friends are, and what they think is important to talk about. When an ambulance flies by us, we always pull over and pray for the suffering person inside. This small act is one that has stuck with me from my childhood. Passing on prayer habits is a great way to bring generations together.

*Be a person of hope.* As it says in 1 Peter 3:15, "Always be ready to give an explanation to anyone who asks you for a reason for your hope." Notice that we are called not to argue, but to witness to hope. We are a Church of mercy and second chances. Of course we do need to be able to articulate what we believe with confidence and kindness in order to lead people to the Source of all mercy, Jesus. If you aren't sure how to do this, consult with your local pastor or reputable Catholic websites. If you don't know of a reason to hope, it's not too late to discover it in faith!

*Donate Catholic books to others.* I have built a small library of Catholic books, and when I no longer need them I donate them to friends or a parish library. Inspiring books sitting on a shelf collecting dust don't help anyone.

If you've found a particular book to be especially helpful, consider buying copies of the book to give away. Michele and I have given away dozens of Fr. Michael Gaitley's book *Consoling the Heart of Jesus*. When we run out, I tell my husband, "Jesus needs me to order some more books." Some people buy the book from me; those who can't afford it get the book for free, so they too can learn about Divine Mercy. God always blesses us when we help others to learn about the Faith.

*Read your children good stories.* Thanks to our Catholic Faith we have a whole directory of saints who are inspiring and well worth learning from as role models in how to reach out to others! On long car trips or at bedtime we use an audiobook called *Truth and Life Dramatized Audio Bible* (www.truthandlifeapp.com) that really makes Bible stories come alive. With our older children, we can read together and share the recent writings of our Holy Father and discuss them around the dinner table. Pope Francis has been an amazing witness to us on sharing the teachings of the Catholic Church with charity.[4]

*Serve in positions of leadership.* When we are willing to serve the community at large, we can be Christ's hands and feet in a broader way, whether you are chairing a fundraising event for your local soup kitchen or organizing a special event for your child's school. Leadership and our Catholic Faith go hand in hand. Simply volunteering at a local Catholic Vacation Bible School is a great way to get involved in instructing children in the Faith and presenting it in a fun way. No matter what position you assume, it all supports the mission.

## Admonish the Sinner

> Today, when I warned a certain young lady that
> she should not be standing for hours in the corri-
> dor with the men, because it was unbecoming for
> a well-bred young lady to do so, she apologized
> and promised to correct herself. . . . I said what I
> had to say. (919)

This story shows a different side of Sr. Faustina, who
was not accustomed to admonishing people for their
behavior as she did with this "certain young lady."
Uncomfortable with the situation this young lady was
in, Faustina felt compelled by her love for this girl to
protect her from harm.

It is our job as parents not only to instruct our
children, but to admonish them, gently and earnestly
reminding them of their duties and obligations and
giving advice or encouragement as needed. That's just
good parenting! Timing is key, of course. I have learned
the hard way that we need to discern carefully when
a child needs correction. A friend recently shared her
story with me, of how her father found a unique way
to challenge her to do the right thing . . . at a time when
she most needed his advice:

> I still remember a time I needed to be admonished
> as a teenage girl. It took place when my dad and I
> were on a long-distance run about three miles from
> the house and my father brought up the subject
> of my "boyfriend." It was a great way for me to
> listen and not "run away" from the conversation,
> since quite frankly, I was too tired to sprint off. He
> shared with me exactly where my parents were
> coming from and I am thankful for their honesty

now. I think that having this conversation on a run was a great match for my personality.

The world is a bit upside down on the message it is sending to our children. Society can give the impression to young people that life is one big party, day and night. This can make living the Christian life and helping others see through this cultural bias a bit challenging. On occasion I have felt called to "admonish" the behavior of others whom I didn't know very well. Each time I did it, I tried to focus on building a bridge and providing a new perspective for them to consider. For example, the other day a neighbor friend kept taking the Lord's name in vain. I kindly told her, in our house, we only use the Lord's name when we pray.

When we decide to intervene and admonish, as Sr. Faustina did, it must always be done with love and with the help of the Holy Spirit. If we "over-admonish" in our own homes, we can create a negative and cold environment. And yet if we never do it, our children will be left to be parented by the world's standards. Our approach should be marked by *charity, clarity,* and *kindness.*

*Admonish with charity.* When we speak with charity, always extending mercy and forgiveness, we will actually strengthen our bond with our children. Sr. Faustina ends her description of the encounter with the young lady with "I said what I had to say." As parents, we sometimes need to do exactly that.

*Admonish with clarity.* Cool down from the shock of what you have heard or witnessed before you speak, so you do not react out of emotions and can articulate your thoughts clearly and fairly. Say no more than you have to.

*Admonish with kindness*. Gentle humor can help to lighten the situation, keep perspective on the matter, and keep the lines of communication open. As parents we encounter a lot of strange and funny situations with our children. Remember—you may need to admonish them, but a light chuckle reminds everyone that affection underlies the conversation.

## Comfort the Sorrowful

> Jesus is bidding me to comfort and reassure a certain soul who has opened herself to me and told me about her difficulties. This soul is pleasing to the Lord, but she is not aware of it. God is keeping her in deep humility. I have carried out the Lord's directives. (1063)

Sorrow is a powerful emotion that can either unite us to the Cross of Christ or launch us into darkness and depression. Ecclesiastes 3:4 tells us that there is "a time to weep and a time to laugh, a time to mourn and a time to dance." When others are in a season of mourning and weeping, it is our job as people of Christ to reach out to them and provide them comfort.

We can walk with the sorrowful by reaching out a helping hand and doing what we can to brighten their day. Forming a relationship is an essential part of providing mercy to others who are in a season of weeping and mourning. As Christ does in the Divine Mercy Image, we too must step toward the person who is in sorrow and allow Christ to use our hearts to penetrate theirs.

I once asked a friend who had buried both her parents within a stretch of four years what had meant the most to her during that dark season of sorrow. She said that a member of our Bible study group had sent her daily Scripture texts for months; that thoughtful mercy had gotten her through her "dark night."

*Perform acts of service.* To console someone who is struggling with grief or depression, head over and help clean if you have the time, especially before family comes into town; or gather a group of families together to cover a one-time cleaning service to deep clean the house. Drop off groceries, so that they have a stocked refrigerator. Set up a calendar and recruit families in the local community to bring dinner to the family. This can be done using an online meal train website or by a sending an e-mail to a group of classmates or friends who might be able to help.

When the Christian community aids us in picking up our cross and carrying our load it is a real sign of God's love.

*Acknowledge those who suffer miscarriage.* The pain and suffering due to a miscarriage are unique because oftentimes it is a private sorrow; others may not even know about the loss. Sending a simple note acknowledging the miscarriage can be a source of great comfort. I also refer families to a local Catholic organization called Back in His Arms Again (www.backinhisarmsagain.com), which focuses on healing and helping families and providing a proper burial for these young children of God.

Another simple (and free) way to provide a touching memorial is to have the baby's name inscribed in the "Book of Life" at the Shrine of the Holy Innocents in New York City (www.innocents.com/shrine.asp). The shrine is dedicated to children who have died before birth and a candle is always lit in their memory. The shrine will send an e-mail to the parents with a Certificate of Life attached in memory of their child.

*Send away for rosary keepsakes.* One practical way to comfort someone who is mourning the loss of a loved one is to have a rosary made from the flower petals from the funeral. I usually ask the funeral director to save a few flowers for me after the wake; I send them to Little Flower Keepsakes, a company that fashions the flowers into beautiful rosaries that will last for a lifetime and encourage prayers for the living and the dead (another work of mercy).[5]

*Join the bereavement committee of your parish.* Many parishes host the funeral luncheon for the family of the deceased. The dishes are provided by parishioners who are part of the committee. I know many young mothers who drop dishes off when asked. A local priest told me that this is an important way to comfort the sorrowful.

*Build bridges with those who are alone.* Spending time with a widow or widower is another way we can be consoling. No matter how long a widower or widow has endured the loss of a spouse, this pain does not go away, and they often spend the majority of their time alone. Consider asking your local pastor to introduce you to those elderly who might enjoy being included at a special gathering, even if you just bring cookies or share a donut after Mass together in the parish hall. Their wisdom is the perfect balm for young, stressed-out mothers, as they share their experiences and provide us the proper perspective we desperately need when motherhood gets overwhelming.

### Forgive All Injuries

> He who knows how to forgive prepares for himself many graces from God. As often as I look upon the cross, so often will I forgive with all my heart. (390)

On Sunday, March 12, 2000, Pope John Paul II offered a worldwide apology for more than two thousand years of offenses committed in the name of the Catholic Faith:

> *Let us forgive and ask forgiveness!* Let us ask pardon for the divisions which have occurred among Christians, for the violence some have used in the service of the truth and for the distrustful and hostile attitudes sometimes taken towards the followers of other religions.[6]

As our frail, Parkinson's-inflicted Holy Father spoke from the high altar of St. Peter's Basilica in Rome, his sincere contrition moved hearts, including many outside the Church. This powerful example of forgiveness shows us what kind of Catholics we need to be: able to forgive others, seek out forgiveness, and forgive ourselves for our mistakes as mothers.

Moments like this one remind us that we can offer healing to others outside our families, even on a worldwide scale. When we encounter a person wounded by a representative of the Catholic Church, our job is to articulate a message of honesty and humility so that they can begin to look past the mistakes of her members and see the beauty and truth of the Church, the Bride of Christ.

In Matthew 5:14 Jesus states, "You are the light of the world. A city set on a mountain cannot be hidden." Sharing this powerful story of forgiveness reminds us that we are called to be a light in the world, to be people of forgiveness to others.

*Be a forgiving parent.* We all need to cultivate hearts of mercy. Our children and family members will hurt, offend, and embarrass us. The response we choose is essential. We must be willing to show mercy to our families and forgive them with a sincere heart, for a grudge held over someone's head will not bear fruits of joy and peace, but rather of wrath and anger. By forgiving, we show others one of the most beautiful attributes of God—his mercy, which flows forth from his most Sacred Heart. We must be willing to be witnesses to mercy, to keep purifying our hearts by forgiving others.

*Seek out forgiveness.* Saying "I'm sorry" can be a really difficult thing to do. I think one of the most frequent reprimands of a mother to her children is "Say you're sorry"—and when the requested apology comes out in an uncharitable way we have to repeat ourselves and command, "Say it like you mean it." However, I often need to heed my own advice. When I have an outburst of anger and offend my children, my spouse, or my friends, I too need to verbalize my contrition.

*Receive Reconciliation.* The sacrament of Reconciliation is a powerful instrument of grace and healing for the family and the greater community. When we attend as a family, our children see we all wound each other and God and need forgiveness. As parents, our job is to encourage our children to overcome the difficulty of going to confession and remind them that the priest is only a screen for Jesus (see 1725). St. Faustina records Jesus' words in the *Diary:* **"When you approach the confessional, know this, that I Myself am waiting there for you. I am only hidden by the priest, but I Myself act in your soul. Here the misery of the soul meets the God of mercy"** (1602).

## Bear Wrongs Patiently

During Meditation, the sister on the kneeler next to mine keeps coughing and clearing her throat, sometimes without a break. It occurred to me once that I might take another place for the time of meditation. . . . But I then I thought that if I did change my place, the sister would notice this and might feel hurt that I had moved away from her. So I decided to continue in prayer in my usual place, and to offer this act of patience to God. Toward the end of the meditation, my soul was flooded with God's consolation, and this to the limit of what my heart could bear; and the Lord gave me to know that if I had moved away from that sister I would have moved away also from those graces that flowed into my soul. (1311)

This *Diary* entry is a powerful reminder for mothers to pray through distractions. Our children can be like flashing lights or blaring sirens at Mass, no matter how hard we try to keep them quiet in the pew. As we humbly endure these difficult times, we can ask the Lord for the graces we need to parent with patience. If we can train our minds to pray despite being distracted we will be able to be "flooded with God's consolation"! Distraction and parenting go hand in hand, but the reality is that where distractions lie, graces abound for us to continue to grow in holiness.

*Seek out opportunities to practice patience.* As life progresses, it is easy to forget about the many challenges of raising young children and to fall into the temptation to avoid opportunities to be distracted once that stage has passed. This is true no matter what stage of life you are in. If we can "embrace" our distractions, whether they be from our own children, the children in front of us in Mass, or the person coughing to our right or left, we can be better Christians by showing charity. If we see that Christ wants us to be charitable first and foremost, we will learn this valid lesson from St. Faustina. Life is full of negative distractions. The experience of being the source of distraction, such that others want to flee from my family during Mass, has left me with a greater desire to be charitable to others experiencing difficult times. Instead of judging others for their lack of courtesy, I now just pray for more graces for the situation at hand.

St. Faustina writes in her *Diary*:

> At those times when I suffer much, I try to remain silent, as I do not trust my tongue which, at such moments, is inclined to talk for itself, while its duty is to help me praise God for all the blessings and gifts which He has given me. . . . The soul will

not attain sanctity if it does not keep watch over its tongue. (92)

*Trust in God's grace.* Our children are not perfect, and they are on a spiritual journey too. We must trust that God is working in our children's hearts while we do our very best to instruct them and raise them. This spiritual work requires patience, tenderness, sensitivity, and love. We need to be better parents than we ever thought we were capable of being. Showing unconditional love is important when family members are suffering in sin.

*Think before you speak (or post).* This is the key to bearing wrongs patiently! Once we start to head down the road of negativity and gossip it is hard to turn back at first. Taking time out to think gives us a chance to calm down, gain control of our emotions, and not let our negative impulses get the best of us. How many times do I leave a conversation telling the Lord, once again, that I am sorry for the words I have just spoken? Sometimes it is best to remain silent.

*Listen to the Holy Spirit.* I've learned that sometimes it is best to wait for a "Holy Spirit moment" before speaking to the person who I feel has wronged me. If you approach the other person out of pride or some self-serving motive, it likely will not end well.

### Pray for the Living and the Dead

Today Sister Jolanta asked me to make an agreement with her: she will pray for me, and I am to

pray for the girls in her class in Vilnius. . . . Our
friendship has deepened. (1171)

In the last chapter, Michele shared about the gift of
offering a Mass card when a loved one dies. Most people think of this when people die, but the reality is that
you can have a Mass offered for a living soul too. An
extended family member once gave me one as a gift
for Christmas, and I was very touched. And there are
several other simple ways to unite your prayers on
behalf of the living and the dead to the prayers of the
whole Church.

*Send Mass cards.* Masses can be said for healing or for
the intentions of the person on any occasion: birthday,
wedding, Baptism, First Communion, Confirmation,
and even special feast days. I am always pleasantly
surprised at people's reactions to receiving a Mass card
for their intention. One of my favorite gifts to give for
a Baptism is an enrollment from the Marians of the
Immaculate Conception. It includes membership in
their spiritual benefit society, which means that the
Marians will pray for you and anyone you enroll in all
their daily Masses, Rosaries, and good works. People
are often moved more by this gift of prayer than by
anything material I have ever given as a gift. In the
words of St. Faustina:

> Oh, what awesome mysteries take place during
> Mass! A great mystery is accomplished in the Holy
> Mass. With what great devotion should we listen
> to and take part in this death of Jesus. One day we
> will know what God is doing for us in each Mass,
> and what sort of gift He is preparing in it for us.

Only His divine love could permit that such a gift
be provided for us. (914)

*Give spiritual bouquets.* Spiritual bouquets are prayers or
devotional acts (such as the Chaplet of Divine Mercy)
that you or a group of friends can offer for someone
else to express joy, sorrow, or best wishes on a special
occasion. Michele and her seven siblings give their parents a spiritual bouquet as a birthday gift every year.
Each sibling picks a day of the birthday month to offer
a special prayer or devotion such as Mass, a Rosary,
a Chaplet of Divine Mercy, or an hour of Eucharistic Adoration for their parents' intentions. They write
their spiritual commitment on a personalized photo
card and display it in a vase or picture frame.

A spiritual bouquet doesn't have to be this elaborate, though. A simple card is a great way to offer a
collection of prayers for someone from a classroom, a
school, a family, or a group of friends. Spiritual bouquets are a concrete way to show a person in need of
prayers that the community is praying.

*Make prayer bracelets.* A friend of ours recently handcrafted rosary bracelets to remind us to pray for our
sick friend every day. Although my intentions are
always good when I promise prayers to someone, I'll
admit that I can forget as time goes on. With a physical
reminder on my wrist, every time I brush the bracelet
up against something or catch a glimpse of it out of the
corner of my eye it reminds me to say a short prayer
for that person. Even though our friend is now healed,
I wear the bracelet when I want to remember to pray
for another friend in a special way.

*Carry prayer cards.* After attending a funeral or a wake, I tuck the prayer card or program from the funeral home into my prayer book. When I go to church I use the cards as a reminder to pray for the deceased person and their family. I have also received prayer cards as a reminder to pray for those who are sick. A woman at my church had small cards made of a certain prayer seeking the intercession of a particular saint for her sick daughter's healing. My kids and I learned a new prayer just by reciting the prayer from the card every morning on the way to school.

*Create a do-it-yourself children's prayer book.* When my children were little, I put together a simple little prayer book to help them during Mass. I used a small photo book (about twenty-five pages) and filled it with prayer cards, family pictures, and the names of people we were praying for. It sat at the bottom of my diaper bag, and I would pull it out during Mass to keep the little ones quiet. This prayer book was a great place to file the Mass cards and holy cards the children received from others.

Motherhood and the spiritual works of mercy go hand in hand. Practicing the spiritual works of mercy is a powerful way for us to connect with those in need. When we are open to being instruments for the Lord, we will have the "eyes to see and ears to hear" (Mt 13:16-17) what Christ is asking of us in every moment. Once you begin to practice these spiritual works consciously, you will receive spiritual benefit and satisfaction in knowing you helped others. Jesus said, "Your light must shine before others, that they may see your good deeds and glorify your heavenly Father" (Mt

5:16). We can only shine when our good works are united with true charity for others.

### *Respond to God's Call in Deed, Word, and Prayer*

*Deed*: These spiritual works of mercy challenge us to see the face of Christ in those around you. This week, perform an act of mercy for someone who is doubtful, lonely, or grieving.

*Word*: Don't complain at all today. Reread the quotation about controlling your tongue in the section Bear Wrongs Patiently (see page 79).

*Prayer*: As you move forward with humility in reaching out to your suffering neighbors, pray with us these words from St. Faustina's *Diary*:

> O Holy Trinity, Eternal God, I want to shine in the crown of Your mercy as a tiny gem whose beauty depends on the ray of Your light and of Your inscrutable mercy. All that is beautiful in my soul is Yours, O God; of myself, I am ever nothing. (617)

CHAPTER 6

# Mary,
# Mother of Mercy

Smiling at me She said to me, *My Daughter, at God's command I am to be, in a special and exclusive way your Mother; but I desire that you, too, in a special way, be My child.* (1414)

The above words from St. Faustina's *Diary* summarize the special role of the Blessed Virgin Mary, Mother of Mercy, in her life. Although most of what is popularly known about the devotion to the Divine Mercy comes from Faustina's visions of Jesus, the Blessed Mother also appeared several times to speak to her and guide her.

Faustina had a great love of the Blessed Mother from childhood. Her order was entrusted to Mary, Mother of Mercy,[1] a title given to Mary in ancient times because she was the vessel that brought mercy into the world and her Son, Jesus, is the revelation of God's mercy.[2] Faustina looked to Mary as her true mother. She strove to imitate her, and asked her to "guard the purity of her heart, soul and body" (874). She wrote in the *Diary*, "O sweet Mother of God, I model my life on you" (1232).

Faustina knew that the secret to a deep interior life was allowing Our Lady to teach her to trust in Jesus because Mary's life was the perfect example of trust.[3] Mary trusted in God's plan of salvation and gave her yes to him. Through Mary's fiat, we are able to receive God's mercy in the person of Jesus Christ! St. Faustina writes in the *Diary*, "Through Her, as through a pure crystal, Your mercy was passed on to us" (1746).

The Blessed Mother told St. Faustina, "*I am . . . the Mother of Mercy and your Mother*" (330), and promised St. Faustina she would give her the grace to be able to do all that God asked of her in her duties without leaving her deep interior union with Christ (785). St. Faustina knew that Mary trusted even in times of difficulty and sorrow. As she too struggled, she wrote in the *Diary*, "Because I am so weak and inexperienced, I nestle like a little child close to [Mary's] heart" (1097).

## Coming to Know and Love the Blessed Mother

I (Michele) have learned that the secret to living out mercy and trust as a wife and mother lies in the imitation and love of the Blessed Mother. Looking back on my faith journey, I can clearly see the motherly hand of Mary, guiding me to her Son. Although I did not fully understand the role of Mary in my life, her influence started when I was a little girl. My parents experienced a deep conversion when I was in second grade. I'll

never forget their decision to start having the family
pray the Rosary every night during Lent that year. But
what I thought was going to be a little Lenten devotion
didn't end—we started praying the Rosary in 1985, and
my parents have done it every night for the past thirty
years. It wasn't always peaceful or easy with eight children, and there was certainly a lot of complaining, but
my parents persevered.

I'll admit that I didn't like praying the Rosary as
a child. It was too long and boring. Yet this familiar
meditative prayer has become an integral part of my
prayer life. When I was about thirteen my parents had
us do the Total Consecration to Mary of St. Louis de
Montfort. If you aren't familiar with the Total Consecration, it's thirty-three days of prayers, Rosaries, and
novenas written in old English to prepare your heart
to consecrate yourself to Jesus through Mary. St. Louis
de Montfort wrote that it is "an easy short, perfect and
secure way of attaining union with our Lord."[4] I did
not think there was anything short about it. This was
longer than the Rosary! Some days you had to say
all these long prayers *and* a Rosary. At the end of the
consecration preparation, you had to write out a long
prayer and sign it. I remember purposely writing it
as sloppily as I could and skipping sentences to get it
done as quickly as possible.

Yet even through my resistance to the prayers, the
graces were able to seep into my soul. I grew to love
Our Lady, and even though I may not have wanted to
participate in some of our family devotions, I knew I
could always turn to her in prayer when I needed help.
My parents put a large picture of the Blessed Mother
in my room after we went on a Marian pilgrimage in

the early 1990s. I would often sit in my bed and just talk to Mary as though she were in the room with me. The eyes on that picture were so real, it was as though she was really looking at me, and I could almost see her smile change when I spoke to her.

To me, Mary exemplified what this book is all about—mercy. She looked at me with tenderness and spoke to my heart as she did to St. Faustina's, and I knew that I, too, was her special child. Then she brought me to her Son as she always does and taught me how to love and know him as only she knew how.

Now I have a special relationship with the Blessed Mother, and by imitating her I can more fully live out my vocation of motherhood. As l look back to some of the most difficult times in my life, I see that her motherly mantle has covered me. It was through reconsecrating myself to her and embracing her trusting heart that I found the trust and peace I experienced during Jacob's illness.

## Mary Understands and Shares Our Suffering

Many women struggle in their relationship with the Blessed Mother. Some women have had a difficult relationship with their own earthly mother. Some grew up in a faith that taught loving Mary was "worshiping" her. Others may get caught up in counting the Hail Marys and novenas or they think that Mary is too perfect in her sinless state to even relate to. One friend commented to me, "Mary only had one kid. She wasn't chasing a toddler while nursing a baby and helping the six-year-old learn to read. How can she know what I am going through?" Yet Mary knows our suffering; her promise to St. Faustina is to all of us:

*I know how much you suffer, but do not be afraid. I
share with you your suffering, and I shall always do
so.* (25)

Although the Blessed Mother was sinless, she
endured human pain, suffering, and struggles. If we
read the gospels, we see that she did not lead a life of
luxury. On the contrary, her life was full of challenges.
Imagine how difficult it was for her to tell Joseph she
was pregnant by the Holy Spirit and then immediately
set out to visit her cousin Elizabeth to help take care
of her in the last months of Elizabeth's pregnancy. I
don't know about you, but the last thing I want to do
when I am feeling the exhaustion of pregnancy is wait
on someone else!

She had to leave her home in the ninth month of
her pregnancy to travel to Bethlehem on a donkey, and
when she had to deliver baby Jesus, there was no place
to lay him except in a dirty animal feeding trough.
When she presented Jesus in the Temple, we read in
Luke 2:35, she was told, "And you yourself a sword
will pierce."

Can you imagine the priest telling you that on your
child's baptismal day?

Then she and St. Joseph had to flee to Egypt to
escape Herod's jealous killing. Mary also suffered
when she lost Jesus in the Temple for three days. Some
of the few recorded words of Mary in the gospels are
"Son, why have you done this to us? Your father and
I have been looking for you with great anxiety" (Lk
2:48). I am sure most mothers have experienced losing
a child in the grocery store or even in a sea of people
at the pool and understand the panic it incites! After

finding Jesus, Luke goes on to say, "his mother kept all these things in her heart" (Lk 2:51).

Mary's deepest suffering was enduring the Passion and death of her Son. In the words of Pope Francis, Mary lived the Passion "to the depths of her soul" in her solidarity with her son in the "martyrdom of the Cross."[5]

Through obedience to the Word of God Mary accepted her lofty yet not easy vocation as wife and mother in the family of Nazareth. Mary understands the vocation of motherhood, and she can help us live mercy in our vocations if we ask her to be with us. We can bring Mary into our lives by honoring her and by incorporating her into our family life.

## Honoring and Imitating the Perfect Mother

My kids have always enjoyed going to new churches and hearing stories of the different images of Mary. As a mother, I draw strength from learning of the graces Mary bestows on her children. While researching this book, I read that the Image of Divine Mercy was first shared with the world in Vilnius, Lithuania, a city already under the patronage and protection of Our Lady of the Gate of Dawn, known to Poles as Our Lady of Ostra Brama.

This image of Our Lady is an icon from the first half of the seventeenth century depicting Mary and the infant Jesus that was placed above one of the city's nine gates for protection against attack. Our Lady of Ostra Brama is venerated throughout both Poland and Lithuania for the miracles, both military and personal, attributed to the intercession of Our Lady. Mary had prepared Vilnius for three hundred years before the

Divine Mercy Image was shared with the world from that same gate.

When my mother (who is 100 percent Polish) glanced down at my notes, she not only recognized the image of the icon immediately, but knew of a local shrine that had a chapel dedicated to Our Lady of Ostra Brama just twenty minutes away. The next day she and I took my kids to the shrine to see the large painting, which sits above a beautiful golden tabernacle, and we all prayed together. It was one of the highlights of the weekend.

We can live out our vocations as mothers by imitating the Blessed Mother. We are called to be meek and humble like Mary. By her faithfulness, she was able completely fulfill her role as the Mother of God. Mary took ordinary tasks, like those we do each day as mothers, and with God's grace made them extraordinary. She never walked on water, turned water into wine, or performed any earthly miracles. Yet she was always where she needed to be, advocating for others and serving as a faithful witness to the Lord. The Blessed Mother is our role model.

There has only been one perfect mom, and that is Mary—Jesus's mother. She is the "New Eve" and provides us with the perfect example of motherhood. As opposed to Eve, who led Adam to fall in the garden, Mary was the perfect woman: obedient, humble, and having the grace to perfectly live out the will of God in her life. Her yes shows us how we can say yes to God in our daily lives by serving our families with love. We can be saints by just living out the ordinariness of motherhood. Cooking, cleaning, and working, all while caring for our children, can be sanctifying.

As St. Teresa of Ávila once wrote, "The Lord walks among the pots and pans helping you interiorly and exteriorly."[6]

Part of emulating Mary is trusting that our duties and tasks done with a meek and humble heart will have eternal value. Our jewels and diamonds in heaven will be our virtues and kind deeds for others here on Earth. Mary is an amazing role model, not only for yourself but for your children.

## Mother of Us All

As Catholics we also look to the Blessed Mother for tender love and intercession. Mary is not only Christ's mother, but our mother too. As Jesus was dying on the Cross, he gave his mother to his beloved disciple with these tender words: "Behold, your mother" (Jn 19:27). The good news is that we too received the Blessed Mother at the foot of the Cross, and when we are attempting to die to ourselves within our vocations, Mary is right there with us. Mary's love is in perfect union with the Holy Spirit; I oftentimes think how much of her tenderness and kindness I lack. As mothers we must take Mary into our hearts to help us parent our children. She stands with us through the good and bad. She knows us and desires to give us Jesus her Son to help us.

If you honor her as your mother, your family will experience her love. *The Catechism of the Catholic Church* describes devotion to the Blessed Mother as "intrinsic to Christian worship." She is the one "to whose protection the faithful fly in all their dangers and needs" (*CCC* 971). When we entrust all our deeds and prayers through her intercession, Mary receives them and presents them to her Son.

Consecrate yourself to her. You can pray the simple Act of Consecration to Mary found at the end of this chapter and in Appendix 1; undertake the formal thirty-three–day preparation my parents had our family do; or look into a more modern thirty-three–day preparation at www.marianconsecration.org. You can also consecrate your children to Mary and place them under her protective mantle (see Appendix 1).

Mary is the Mother of Mercy, the perfect mother, and the mother of us all. It is her duty to bring us into the heart of Jesus, the heart that loves us deeply and desires to pour graces upon us as we live out our lives as mothers. Emily and I have both experienced her powerful intercession in our lives as we strive to be more like her each day. We encourage you to begin your journey with Divine Mercy by entrusting yourself to the Blessed Mother. Allow her to take you by the hand and lead you to her Son, so you too can look upon the Image of Divine Mercy, allowing the rays of love to penetrate your soul, and say with your whole heart: "Jesus, I trust in you!"

### Respond to God's Call in Deed, Word, and Prayer

*Deed*: Review the Scriptures on the Blessed Mother's life cited in this chapter. Take some time out to pray about your family's devotion to Mary. Everyone can grow closer to her! Ask the Holy Spirit to show you how you can develop a deeper devotion to our Mother so she can bring you closer to Jesus.

*Word*: Imagine yourself in the heart of Mary. Picture you and your family covered by her mantle and wrapped in her arms. Pen a short prayer to Mary asking her to help you grow in tenderness, compassion, and trust.

*Prayer*: If you feel called to consecrate yourself to Mary, pray this Act of Consecration to Mary:

> Mary, Mother of Jesus and Mother of Mercy, since Jesus from the Cross gave you to me, I take you as my own. And since Jesus gave me to you, take me as your own. Make me docile like Jesus on the Cross, obedient to the Father and trusting in humility and in love.
>
> Mary, my Mother, in imitation of the Father, who gave his Son to you, I too give my all to you, to you I entrust all that I am, all that I have and all that I do.
>
> Help me to surrender ever more fully to the Spirit. Lead me deeper into the Mystery of the Cross and the fullness of the Church. As you formed the heart of Jesus by the Spirit, form my heart to be the throne of Jesus in his glorious coming.[7]

May mercy reign in your home!

# Afterword

I'm sort of embarrassed to admit this, but before reading this book, I encountered St. Faustina and her Divine Mercy devotions most often not in church or by reading her famous *Diary*, but in my laundry room.

Several years ago, in an effort to transform laundry from my most despised domestic chore into a loving act of service for my family, I began to recreate my small workspace into a chapel of sorts. I installed a small CD player where I could listen to spiritual tunes and placed a bulletin board on the wall to hold holy cards and inspirational messages.

One of the first items that I pinned to that board was the Image of Divine Mercy. I had often prayed before the image at our parish and had made repeated attempts to read St. Faustina's amazing *Diary*. But it was there in my laundry room, as I sorted socks or soaked stained uniform shirts, that I finally began to grasp what it was all about. I would peer into Jesus' loving gaze, see those blue and red rays pouring from his Sacred Heart . . . and my eyes would fall upon the words at the bottom of the image:

Jesus, I trust in you.

Even without knowing much about St. Faustina Kowalska or the origins of her Divine Mercy devotion, I was transfixed by those words. When I doubted my worthiness to raise up my sons to become the faithful young Catholic men I so wanted them to be, or grew overwhelmed about the trajectory of my own vocation and apostolate, these five words were a reminder to me to lean into God's mercy. *"Just trust,"* I would tell myself as I looked at the holy card version of that now famous painting. *"God's got this."*

I'm grateful beyond measure to my new spiritual sisters in Christ, Michele Faehnle and Emily Jaminet, for the work they have put into compiling what is truly a gift for today's Catholic moms. By so lovingly and practically introducing us not only to St. Faustina and her devotions, but also to the spiritual and corporal acts of mercy, they have armed us to be on the front lines of a great battle.

We live in a world filled all too often with pain and suffering. In the midst of busy days spent balancing competing priorities, we mothers may question what impact we could possibly have in stemming the rising tide of such hurt. As much as we want to serve others, and to meet the endless rush of physical and emotional demands both inside and outside of our homes, is there really anything we can do to contribute to needed and lasting change?

Blessedly, the book you hold in your hands is a reminder that not only *can* we contribute, but that our work on mercy's front lines holds perhaps the very keys to the fundamental changes needed to spread God's saving love in our world. Emily and Michele have not only taught us simple yet profound devotions to share with our families. They have taught us how—in word, deed, and prayer—to become Christ's eyes, ears, mouth, hands, and feet by living out the corporal and spiritual acts of mercy in our homes and communities. Our children and spouses must never be our "excuse" for not being agents of mercy. They are instead our partners in pouring God's loving mercy on a world desperately in need.

Does that seem overwhelming to you, even after reading this lovely book? Please know that you are never alone. The Blessed Mother, St. Faustina, St. John Paul II, and an army of spiritual companions are journeying with you toward Christ, and now you also have Michele, Emily, and me inviting you into a circle of spiritual sisterhood at *CatholicMom.com*. If the demands of your vocation feel overwhelming, if your prayer life feels dry or even nonexistent, or if you question the value of what you are doing with your life, please remember that the work you do daily as a wife and mother is a beautiful and worthy act of mercy. I invite you to join moms around the world in carrying the message of Divine Mercy in your heart. Through us, God will shower his loving mercy upon our world.

Lisa M. Hendey
Founder of *CatholicMom.com*
and author of *The Grace of Yes*

# Appendix 1
# Prayers

## A Prayer for Divine Transformation from Within (163)

+ O Most Holy Trinity! As many times as I breathe, as many times as my heart beats, as many times as my blood pulsates through my body, so many thousand times do I want to glorify Your mercy.

+ I want to be completely transformed into Your mercy and to be Your living reflection, O Lord. May the greatest of all divine attributes, that of Your unfathomable mercy, pass through my heart and soul to my neighbor.

Help me, O Lord, that my eyes may be merciful, so that I may never suspect or judge from appearances, but look for what is beautiful in my neighbors' souls and come to their rescue.

Help me, that my ears may be merciful, so that I may give heed to my neighbors' needs and not be indifferent to their pains and moanings.

Help me, O Lord, that my tongue may be merciful, so that I should never speak negatively of my neighbor, but have a word of comfort and forgiveness for all.

Help me, O Lord, that my hands may be merciful and filled with good deeds, so that I may do only good to my neighbors and take upon myself the more difficult and toilsome tasks.

Help me, that my feet may be merciful, so that I may hurry to assist my neighbor, overcoming my own fatigue and weariness. My true rest is in the service of my neighbor.

Help me, O Lord, that my heart may be merciful so that I myself may feel all the sufferings of my neighbor. I will refuse my heart to no one. I will be sincere even with those who, I know, will abuse my kindness. And I will lock myself up in the most merciful Heart of Jesus. I will bear my own suffering in silence. May Your mercy, O Lord, rest upon me.

## The Chaplet of Divine Mercy

"The Chaplet of Divine Mercy" is recited using ordinary rosary beads. It is preceded by two opening prayers from the *Diary* of St. Faustina and followed by a closing prayer.

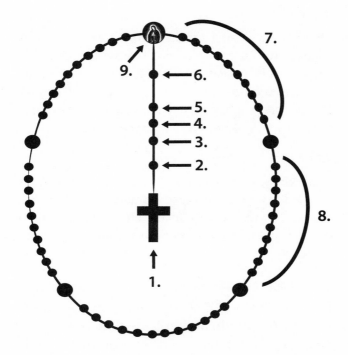

1. *The Sign of the Cross*

   In the name of the Father, and of the Son, and of the Holy Spirit. Amen.

2. *Optional Opening Prayers*

   You expired, Jesus, but the source of life gushed forth for souls, and the ocean of mercy opened up for the whole world. O Fount of Life, unfathomable Divine Mercy, envelope the whole world and empty Yourself out upon us.

   *(Repeat three times)* O Blood and Water, which gushed forth from the Heart of Jesus as a fountain of Mercy for us, I trust in You!

3. *Our Father*

> Our Father, Who art in heaven, hallowed be Thy name; Thy kingdom come; Thy will be done on earth as it is in heaven. Give us this day our daily bread; and forgive us our trespasses as we forgive those who trespass against us; and lead us not into temptation, but deliver us from evil. Amen.

4. *Hail Mary*

> Hail Mary, full of grace. The Lord is with thee. Blessed art thou amongst women, and blessed is the fruit of thy womb, Jesus. Holy Mary, Mother of God, pray for us sinners, now and at the hour of our death. Amen.

5. *The Apostles' Creed*

> I believe in God, the Father almighty, Creator of heaven and earth, and in Jesus Christ, His only Son, our Lord, who was conceived by the Holy Spirit, born of the Virgin Mary, suffered under Pontius Pilate, was crucified, died and was buried; He descended into hell; on the third day He rose again from the dead; He ascended into heaven, and is seated at the right hand of God the Father almighty; from there He will come to judge the living and the dead. I believe in the Holy Spirit, the holy catholic Church, the Communion of Saints, the forgiveness of sins, the resurrection of the body, and life everlasting. Amen.

6. *The Eternal Father*

> Eternal Father, I offer you the Body and Blood, Soul and Divinity of Your dearly beloved Son, Our Lord, Jesus Christ, in atonement for our sins and those of the whole world.

7. *On the ten small beads of each decade:*

   For the sake of His sorrowful Passion have mercy on us and on the whole world.

8. *Repeat for the remaining decades:*

   Say the Eternal Father (6) on the Our Father beads and then ten "For the sake of His sorrowful Passion" (7) on the following Hail Mary beads.

9. *Holy God*

   *(Repeat three times)* Holy God, Holy Mighty One, Holy Immortal One, have mercy on us and on the whole world.

10. *Optional Closing Prayer*

    Eternal God, in whom mercy is endless and the treasury of compassion—inexhaustible, look kindly upon us and increase Your mercy in us, that in difficult moments we might not despair nor become despondent, but with great confidence submit ourselves to Your holy will, which is Love and Mercy itself.

# The Rosary

The Rosary is a Scripture-based prayer conceived in the thirteenth century. It begins with the Apostles' Creed, which summarizes the great mysteries of the Catholic Faith. The Our Father, which introduces each mystery, is from the gospels (Mt 6:9–13). The first part of the Hail Mary comprises the angel Gabriel's words to Mary announcing Christ's birth (Lk 1:28) and Elizabeth's greeting to Mary (Lk 1:42). St. Pius V officially added the second part of the Hail Mary in the sixteenth century. The Mysteries of the Rosary center on the events of Christ's life. There are four sets of Mysteries: the Joyful, Sorrowful, Glorious, and—added by Pope John Paul II in 2002—Luminous.

The repetition in the Rosary is meant to lead one into restful and contemplative prayer related to each Mystery. The gentle repetition of the words helps us to enter into the silence of our hearts, where Christ's spirit dwells. The Rosary can be said privately or with a group.

The Joyful Mysteries are traditionally prayed on Mondays, Saturdays, and the Sundays of Advent:

1. The Annunciation

2. The Visitation

3. The Nativity

4. The Presentation in the Temple

5. The Finding in the Temple

The Sorrowful Mysteries are traditionally prayed on Tuesdays, Fridays, and the Sundays of Lent:

1. The Agony in the Garden

2. The Scourging at the Pillar

3. The Crowning with Thorns

4. The Carrying of the Cross

5. The Crucifixion and Death

The Glorious Mysteries are traditionally prayed on Wednesdays and the Sundays outside of Lent and Advent:

1. The Resurrection
2. The Ascension
3. The Descent of the Holy Spirit
4. The Assumption
5. The Coronation of Mary

The Luminous Mysteries are traditionally prayed on Thursdays:

1. The Baptism of Christ in the Jordan
2. The Wedding Feast at Cana
3. The Proclamation of the Kingdom of God
4. The Transfiguration
5. The Institution of the Eucharist

*Praying the Rosary*

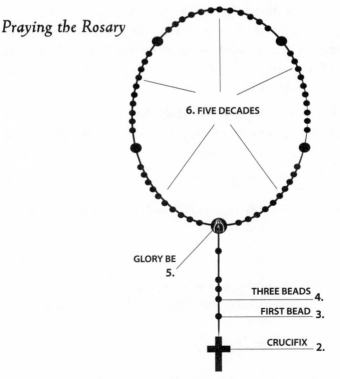

6. FIVE DECADES

GLORY BE
5.

THREE BEADS 4.

FIRST BEAD 3.

CRUCIFIX 2.

1. SIGN OF THE CROSS

Familiarize yourself and / or your group with the prayers of the Rosary.

1.  Make the Sign of the Cross.

2.  Holding the crucifix, say the Apostles' Creed.

3.  On the first bead, say an Our Father.

4.  Say a Hail Mary on each of the next three beads.

5.  Say the Glory Be.

6.  For each of the five decades, announce the Mystery, then say the Our Father.

7.  While fingering each of the ten beads of the decade, next say ten Hail Marys while meditating on the Mystery. Then say a Glory Be. (After the Glory Be, some say the following prayer requested by the Blessed Virgin Mary at Fatima: "O my Jesus, forgive us our sins, save us from the fires of hell, and lead all souls to Heaven, especially those who have most need of thy mercy.")

8.  After finishing the five decades, say the Hail Holy Queen, followed by this prayer and the prayer to St. Michael the Archangel.

    V. Pray for us, O holy Mother of God.

    R. That we may be made worthy of the promises of Christ.

    V. Let us pray.

    R. O God, whose Only Begotten Son, by his life, Death, and Resurrection, has purchased for us the rewards of eternal life, grant, we beseech thee, that while meditating on these mysteries of the most holy Rosary of the Blessed Virgin Mary, we may imitate what they contain and obtain what they promise, through the same Christ our Lord. Amen.

## Hail Holy Queen

Hail, Holy Queen, Mother of Mercy, our life, our sweetness and our hope! To thee do we cry, poor banished children of Eve. To thee do we send up our sighs, mourning and weeping in this valley of tears! Turn, then, O most gracious Advocate, thine eyes of mercy toward us, and after this, our exile, show unto us the blessed fruit of thy womb, Jesus. O clement, O loving, O sweet Virgin Mary.

## Prayer to St. Michael the Archangel

St. Michael the Archangel, defend us in battle. Be our protection against the wickedness and snares of the devil. May God rebuke him, we humbly pray; and do thou, O Prince of the Heavenly Host, by the Divine Power of God, cast into hell Satan and all the evil spirits who prowl throughout the world seeking the ruin of souls.

## Memorare of St. Bernard

Remember, O most gracious Virgin Mary, that never was it known that anyone who fled to thy protection, implored thy help, or sought thine intercession was left unaided.

Inspired by this confidence, I fly unto thee, O Virgin of virgins, my mother; to thee do I come, before thee I stand, sinful and sorrowful. O Mother of the

Word Incarnate, despise not my petitions, but in
thy mercy hear and answer me.

Amen.

# The Stations of the Cross

1. Jesus is condemned to death
2. Jesus carries his Cross
3. Jesus falls the first time
4. Jesus meets his mother
5. Simon of Cyrene helps Jesus carry the Cross
6. Veronica wipes the face of Jesus
7. Jesus falls the second time
8. Jesus meets the women of Jerusalem
9. Jesus falls the third time
10. Jesus is stripped of his garments
11. Crucifixion: Jesus is nailed to the Cross
12. Jesus dies on the Cross
13. Jesus is taken down from the Cross (Deposition or Lamentation)
14. Jesus is laid in the tomb

# Morning Offering

O Jesus, through the Immaculate Heart of Mary, I
offer You my prayers, works,

joys, and sufferings of this day for all the intentions
of Your Sacred Heart,

in union with the Holy Sacrifice of the Mass throughout the world,

in reparation for my sins, for the intentions of all my relatives and friends, and in particular for the intentions of the Holy Father. Amen.

## An Act of Consecration to Mary

Mary, Mother of Jesus and Mother of Mercy, since Jesus from the Cross gave you to me, I take you as my own. And since Jesus gave me to you, take me as your own. Make me docile like Jesus on the Cross, obedient to the Father and trusting in humility and in love. Mary, my Mother, in imitation of the Father, who gave his Son to you, I too give my all to you, to you I entrust all that I am, all that I have and all that I do. Help me to surrender ever more fully to the Spirit. Lead me deeper into the Mystery of the Cross, and the fullness of the Church. As you formed the heart of Jesus by the Spirit, form my heart to be the throne of Jesus in his glorious coming.[1]

## Prayer of Consecration of a Child to Mary

Holy Mary, Mother of God and Mother of all faithful, I place my little child under your mothering protection. To you I completely consecrate him—body and soul. Take him under your care and keep him always. Protect him in his infancy and keep him sound in body and mind. Guard over his youth and keep his heart pure, his thoughts ever holy and directed to God and spiritual things. Protect him always throughout life—in his joys and sorrows, in his dealings with others. Always and in all things be a true mother to him, Mary, and preserve him. I commend him entirely to you. Remember Mother Mary, that through this act of consecration he is by a special claim your child as well as mine; guard him and keep him as your property and possession. Amen.[2]

# Appendix 2
# Thirty Days of Mercy

The Thirty Days of Mercy are daily mini-reflections on motherhood. For each day, we provide a short quotation from the *Diary* of St. Faustina, questions to ponder, and a prayer. After you complete the thirty days, sign up at divinemercyformoms.com to receive more reflections in your inbox.

## Day 1—Joy

It is from the face of God that this joy flows. (1592)

What is your source of daily joy? Do you seek joy in God or in the pleasures of life?

*Dear Jesus, please help me not to bemoan my tasks at hand but rather to see the value they have for you. Help me live with joy. Amen.*

## Day 2—Prayer

With no one else is it so easy to talk as with You, O God. (670)

Do you find it easy to talk with God? Do you spend all day talking with others or yourself? Could you use that time to talk with God?

*Dear Jesus, please teach me how to pray. Help me find it easy to spend my day talking with you. Amen.*

## Day 3—Fortitude

> With God's grace a soul can overcome the greatest
> difficulties. (287)

Do the difficulties and challenges you are faced with
seem overwhelming? Do you trust that God's grace
can help you through these times?

*Dear Jesus, please help me to draw close to you when life
is difficult. Give me the grace I need to be the mother you
want me to be. Amen.*

## Day 4—Prudence

> We should often pray to the Holy Spirit for this
> grace of prudence. (1106).

Do you struggle to know what God is calling you to?
Do you ask the Holy Spirit to help you know what to
do?

*Dear Lord, please help me to find prudence in my daily
life. Send your Holy Spirit and pour out this grace upon
me. Amen.*

## Day 5—Love

> Only love has meaning; it raises up our smallest
> actions into infinity. (502)

Do you combine your daily duties with love and raise
them to eternal actions? How can you grow in love?

*Dear Jesus, please help me to love my family members
consistently and constantly. Help me to do all my activities
for my family out of love. Amen.*

# Day 6—Love of God

I burn with the desire to love Him ever more and more. (525)

How can you deepen your desire to love Christ more? What can you do to keep your eyes fixed on him and not yourself?

*Jesus, please help me to love you with all my heart, mind, and soul. Keep me focused on what my priorities should be today, and purify the love of my heart. Amen.*

# Day 7—Obedience

Jesus, drive away from me the thoughts that are not in accord with your will. (638)

Do you struggle with giving up control? Do you desire the will of God over your own will?

*Lord, please show me how to be more joyful in my obedience. Help me to do your will and not mine. Amen.*

# Day 8—Peace

He said to me, **My daughter, peace be with you.** (1067)

Do you picture yourself as a daughter of Christ? Do you believe that Christ can bring peace to the most difficult of matters?

*Jesus, give me your peace and make my home a peaceful place. Amen.*

# Day 9—Suffering

And the greater the sufferings, the more I see that I am becoming like Jesus. (1394)

When the road in life gets difficult, do you allow your personal sufferings to bring you closer to Christ? How do you deal with stress and suffering?

*Dear Jesus, please console me when I am suffering and teach me how to better follow you on the path to holiness. Amen.*

## Day 10—Resting in the Lord

**Come to Me, all of you.** (1485)

Are you anxious about sharing the Christian message with everyone? How might this hold you back from being a better witness to Christ?

*Lord, may I find true rest in you. Amen.*

## Day 11—Forgiveness

> If someone causes you trouble, think what good you can do for the person who caused you to suffer. (1760)

How do you respond when you are angry? Do you forgive easily, or do you hold grudges? How would Christ want you to respond?

*Dear Jesus, please send me Your Holy Spirit so that I can respond to difficult moments with virtue and keep anger and strife out of my home. Amen.*

## Day 12—Mercy

**From all My wounds, like from streams, mercy flows for souls.** (1190)

What is holding you back today from seeking out Christ's mercy? Hand Christ your woes and ask him to heal you and show you his mercy!

From the Divine Mercy Chaplet: *"For the sake of His sorrowful Passion have mercy on us and on the whole world."* Amen.

## Day 13—Patience

> I have learned that the greatest power is hidden in patience. (1514)

Are you a patient person? What kind of mother would you be if you were more patient?

*Jesus, may you give me the grace to become more virtuous and patient, like your Blessed Mother. Amen.*

## Day 14—Sacrifice

> We do not know the number of souls that is ours to save through our prayers and sacrifices. (1783)

Do you pray for others and offer up your trials for souls who need it? What tasks could you offer up throughout your day so your annoyance turns to purposeful work?

*Dear Jesus, please help me to realize that I can help others in their faith journey by praying and offering up sacrifices. Give me the graces I need to know who you want me to pray for. Amen.*

## Day 15—Contentment

> To suffer without complaining, to bring comfort to others and to drown my own sufferings in the most Sacred Heart of Jesus! (224)

Do you complain a lot to others? Are you content in your vocation of being a wife and mother?

*Dear Jesus, please help me not to complain, and help my children to do the same. Amen.*

## Day 16—Transformation

> I want to be completely transformed into Your mercy and to be Your living reflection, O Lord. (163)

Does being "transformed into Your mercy" scare you or excite you? Who in your life do you need to forgive and seek forgiveness from so that Christ can begin to transform you?

*Dear Jesus, please transform me and my family from the inside out. Amen.*

## Day 17—Strength

> Patience, prayer and silence—these are what give strength to the soul. (944)

Do you find enough prayer and silence in your life? How do you handle it when you don't get enough?

*Dear Jesus, please help me to begin my day with prayer. Please give me a moment of silence that I may spend it with you to grow in strength. Amen.*

## Day 18—Imitating Mary

> The more I imitate the Mother of God, the more deeply I get to know God. (843)

How do you view the Blessed Mother? Do you see her as a vital person in bringing you closer to Christ and desire to imitate her virtues and ways?

*Dear Jesus, make me tenderhearted like your Blessed Mother. Help me to imitate her as I learn to trust in you. Amen.*

## Day 19—Intimacy with Christ

**Snuggle close to My merciful Heart, and I will fill it with peace.** (1074)

Is this how you visualize God? Do you imagine him wanting you to nuzzle close to his heart? How do you attempt to find peace? What does peace mean to you?

*Dear Jesus, help me to see your blessings even when my life feels stormy. Bring me closer to your heart and fill me with peace. Amen.*

## Day 20—Trust

A more pleasing praise to God

Is a soul innocent and filled with childlike trust. (1750)

Do you see your children as a gift to God and as blessings to the whole family? In what ways has motherhood and having children renewed your childlike trust?

*Dear Jesus, help me to be able to leap into your arms with trust as your little child. I want to be a pleasing praise to you. Amen.*

## Day 21—A Delight to the Lord

**My child you are My delight, you are the comfort of My Heart.** (164)

Do you know how special you are in the eyes of God? You delight and comfort him! Take some time to reflect on this unique relationship Christ is offering you.

*Dear Jesus, please teach me how to comfort you with my prayers and actions. Help me to teach my children to be your delight. Amen.*

## Day 22—Virtue

I had many opportunities to practice virtue. (401)

Which virtues are difficult for you? In which areas can you grow so as to improve your witness and create a more peaceful home? The theological virtues are faith, hope, and charity; the cardinal virtues are prudence (sound judgment), justice (fairness), fortitude (courage), and temperance (self-control).

*Dear Jesus, please help me to live a life of virtue. Amen.*

## Day 23—Perseverance

O my Jesus, give me strength to endure. (1740)

In what aspects of your life do you need to persevere? Is it with your own personal faith or your relationships with your family, or do you feel persecuted by others? God wants you to gain strength to endure during difficult times.

*Dear Jesus, please help me to bring my troubles to you. Give me strength to endure the crosses that come my way. Amen.*

## Day 24—Jealousy

Rejoice in the success of others. (241)

What situations make you feel competitive? Where do you need to grow spiritually so you can rejoice in others' success (including other people's children's success)?

*Dear Jesus, please help me not to make bitter comparisons with others. Give me strength to work on making things better instead. Amen.*

## Day 25—Self-Denial

Now I understand well that what unites our soul most closely to God is self-denial. (462)

Do you find it difficult to deny yourself your "favorites"? Can you resist your daily temptations? What items are hard for you? (Sweets, coffee, complaining . . . )

*Dear Jesus, I surrender myself to you. Help me to learn how to offer up the pleasures of the world for you. Amen.*

## Day 26—Sadness

**Daughter, give Me your misery, because it is your exclusive property.** (1318)

What do you do with your trials? Do you share them with God or others or do you cling to your misery?

*Dear Jesus, please help me to open up to you and seek your mercy for the things that weigh me down in life. Amen.*

## Day 27—Courage

**Do not fear anything. I am with you.** (573)

What fears hold you back from loving God? How can you have greater trust?

*Dear Jesus, please help me to trust you and learn what it means to live a holy life. Help me never to fear no matter how dark matters look. Amen.*

## Day 28—Constancy

**O heart, which received Me in the morning and at noon are all ablaze with hatred against Me, hatred of all sorts!** (1702)

When do you "fall off the wagon" in living out your witness as a Christian? Is it with certain friends, family members, coworkers, or other parents?

*Dear Jesus, please help my love for you never to die out or fade away. Amen.*

## Day 29—Strength in Weakness

When the soul is weak, let it ask Jesus Himself to act. (1179)

When you feel burdened and weak, do you ask Jesus to help you? Do you believe he will strengthen you?

*Dear Jesus, I am so weak sometimes. Please be my strength and act in me so that I may be a faithful follower. Amen.*

# Day 30—Thanksgiving

I shall steep myself in a prayer of thanksgiving. (1367)

Do you thank God for your daily blessings? Do you have an "attitude of gratitude"?

*Dear Jesus, thank you for all the blessings you have given me. I have been given so much. Help me to thank you for everything in my life, especially the gift of being a mother. Amen.*

# Study Guide

This guide combines two key topics—motherhood and Divine Mercy as explained by the *Diary* of St. Faustina. St. Faustina has a lot of wisdom for us mothers on how we can deepen our trust in the Lord. And nothing is more fun than learning with friends and soon-to-be friends!

## Instructions for Facilitators

- *Decide where the study group will meet.* Michele and I have participated in studies at different members' houses. We've met in tea houses, restaurants, and coffee shops when no one was able to host in their home. One summer when the children were little we met at a park; the children could play in the grass while we gathered for prayer and fellowship. Meeting at a parish hall or larger gathering place makes it possible to bring in the wider Catholic community.
- *Find a time of day that works for the women involved.* Our local Bible study split into a daytime study and an evening study based on what worked best for the members.
- *Promote your study group.* How are you going to get the word out? Invite your friends; place an announcement in your church bulletin; post it on Facebook.
- *Organize refreshments.* Decide who will bring a small snack or drink. For our studies, the host would

always put out hot water and we would take turns bringing boxes of tea to restock the host's supply. Tea works because it is affordable and you can find a nice variety. Some nights we celebrate with a small glass of wine.

* *Plan the first meeting.* We recommend that everyone purchase the book ahead of time and read the introduction before the first meeting; however, if you provide the books at the first meeting, we suggest reading the introduction aloud as a group. The first meeting is also a great time for all the participants to introduce themselves and share a little bit about who they are and what brought them to this study.

## Introduction

*Opening prayer*: Select an opening prayer from Appendix 1.

1. Have you ever asked for a sign from God for his will in your life? What happened?

2. The book begins with the story of a pilgrimage to the National Shrine of The Divine Mercy. Have you ever taken a pilgrimage to a holy site? If so, share where you have been. Learn more about our favorite pilgrimages at divinemercyformoms.com.

3. Reread the quotation from Pope Francis's Papal Bull *Misericordiae Vultus* on page xviii. What strikes you about this passage?

Close with "A Prayer for Divine Transformation from Within," found in Appendix 1. Ask the group members if they have specific prayer intentions, and pray together for these needs.

## 1. St. Faustina, Apostle of Divine Mercy

**How long shall I put up with you and how long will you keep putting Me off?** (9)

*Opening prayer*: Select an opening prayer from Appendix 1.

1. This chapter begins in Kraków and describes a mountaintop experience, a transforming moment in Michele's life. Have you experienced anything like this in your life?

2. Reread the above quotation from the *Diary*. Can you relate to it? How do you put Christ off? Does it lead to you to happiness?

3. What strikes you most about the life of St. Faustina, described briefly in this chapter? To learn more about St. Faustina, visit www.faustyna.pl/zmbm/en.

4. Pope Francis has spent much of his pontificate speaking about mercy, stating it "is the best thing we can feel: it changes the world." Why do you think this is? How has mercy touched you?

Close with "A Prayer for Divine Transformation from Within." Ask the group members if they have specific prayer intentions, and pray together for these needs.

## 2. Developing Trust in Jesus through the Divine Mercy Devotion

**Encourage the souls with whom you come in contact to trust in My infinite mercy. Oh, how I**

**love those souls who have complete confidence in Me—I will do everything for them.** (294)

*Opening prayer*: Select an opening prayer from Appendix 1.

1. Sr. Faustina had only two years of formal education, yet Jesus asked her to undertake the mission of spreading this great devotion. Do you ever feel unqualified to do the work that God is asking of you? In what ways has the Lord made up for what you lack?

2. Do you trust God? Do you have a difficult time with the concept of letting go and letting God? See the Recommended Resources page on divine-mercyformoms.com for more on this topic.

3. Have you had a time in your life when you had to rely on the Lord and he rescued you? Such an experience can be the spark that begins your deeper conversion to God. Tell your story.

4. What do you think of the Divine Mercy Image? Do you feel Christ reaching out to you?

5. What are some of your more stressful times of your day? Have you ever considered taking time out to pray during the three o'clock hour? Is it difficult to find prayer time in your daily life? Do you picture Christ listening to you?

6. Read the following quotations from the *Diary* and reflect:

   **Tell me all, My Child, hide nothing from Me, because My loving Heart, the Heart of your Best Friend, is listening to you.** (1486)

> **Oh, if souls would only want to listen to My voice when I am speaking in the depths of their hearts, they would reach the peak of holiness in a short time.** (584)

Close with "A Prayer for Divine Transformation from Within." Ask the group members if they have specific prayer intentions and pray together for these needs.

## 3. Showing Mercy to Our Neighbor

> **I am giving you three ways of exercising mercy toward your neighbor: the first—by deed, the second—by word, the third—by prayer. In these three degrees is contained the fullness of mercy, and it is an unquestionable proof of love for Me.** (742)

*Opening prayer*: Select an opening prayer from Appendix 1.

1. Read the articles on Mercy and Sin in the *Catechism* (*CCC* 1846–51). The formula for practicing mercy is almost the opposite of practicing a sinful action. The *Catechism* defines sin as "an offense again reason, truth, and right conscience; it is failure in genuine love for God and neighbor caused by a perverse attachment to certain goods" and as "an utterance, a deed, or a desire contrary to the eternal law" (*CCC* 1849). What connection do you see between the *Catechism's* definition of sin and a merciful deed?

2. Reread the above quotation from the *Diary*. The threefold plan for merciful action is a powerful way to connect with others. Did you know there was a

formula for consciously practicing Divine Mercy to others?

3. Have you ever participated in a merciful deed that was successful like the cake story, in which numerous people worked together on a good deed for the Lord? Share your story.

4. Read Matthew 5:16. What does it mean that "your light must shine before others"? How does what St. Faustina shares with us regarding deed, word, and prayer connect with this Scripture?

Close with "A Prayer for Divine Transformation from Within." Ask the group members if they have specific prayer intentions, and pray together for these needs.

## 4. The Corporal Works of Mercy

> I understand souls who are suffering against hope, for I have gone through that fire myself. But God will not give [us anything] beyond our strength. (386)

*Opening prayer*: Select an opening prayer from Appendix 1.

1. Where do you see the most suffering around you? What is your impression of the corporal works of mercy? Have you evet tried to practice them before?

2. Think of a time you underwent suffering. Did that time bring you closer to the Lord as Jacob's illness did Michele? How has the Lord taken care of you during your trials?

3.  This chapter includes specific ways to bring deeds to life and practice them. Reread the quotations from the *Diary* before each of the corporal works of mercy and discuss each work with regard to living out the quotation.

*The Corporal Works of Mercy*

1.  Feed the hungry.
2.  Give drink to the thirsty.
3.  Clothe the naked.
4.  Shelter the homeless.
5.  Visit the sick.
6.  Visit the imprisoned.
7.  Bury the dead.

Close with "A Prayer for Divine Transformation from Within." Ask the group members if they have specific prayer intentions, and pray together for these needs.

## 5. The Spiritual Works of Mercy

Write this for the many souls who are often worried because they do not have the material means with which to carry out an act of mercy. Yet spiritual mercy, which requires neither permissions nor storehouses, is much more meritorious and is within the grasp of every soul. If a soul does not exercise mercy somehow or other, it will not obtain My mercy on the day of judgment. Oh, if only souls knew how to gather eternal treasure for themselves, they would not be judged, for they would forestall My judgment with their mercy. (1317)

*Opening prayer*: Select an opening prayer from Appendix 1.

1. What do you think of this quotation from the *Diary*? How does it expand your perspective on Divine Mercy?

2. Reread the quotation on spiritual poverty and loneliness from Mother Teresa at the beginning of the chapter. How do you see this to be true in our country?

3. This chapter includes specific ways to bring deeds to life and practice them. Reread the quotations from the *Diary* before each of the spiritual works of mercy and discuss each work with regard to living it out.

*The Spiritual Works of Mercy*

1. Counsel the doubtful.

2. Instruct the ignorant.

3. Admonish sinners.

4. Comfort the afflicted.

5. Forgive offenses.

6. Bear wrongs patiently.

7. Pray for the living and the dead.

Close with "A Prayer for Divine Transformation from Within." Ask the group members if they have specific prayer intentions, and pray together for these needs.

## 6.  Mary, Mother of Mercy

Smiling at me she said to me, *My Daughter, at God's command I am to be, in a special and exclusive way your Mother; but I desire that you, too, in a special way, be my child.* (1414)

*Opening prayer*: Select an opening prayer from Appendix 1.

1.  Reread the quotation from the *Diary*. Do you consider Mary your mother?

2.  Read section 971, Devotion to the Blessed Virgin, of *The Catechism of the Catholic Church*. Is there a specific title for or devotion to Mary that connects you to her?

3.  Have you ever visited a Marian shrine? If so, what was your experience like? If not, ask other group members if there is a shrine in your area you could visit with your family or small group.

4.  How can Mary specifically help you live out mercy in your vocation as a mother?

Close with "A Prayer for Divine Transformation from Within." Ask the group members if they have specific prayer intentions, and pray together for these needs. Pray a decade of the Rosary together.

As this study comes to a close, consider planning a work of mercy you can carry out as a group. Allow the Holy Spirit to show you what he wants you to do. Contact us through our website, divinemercyformoms. com, and share your idea! Be sure to include pictures.

*Example:* A friend in our Bible study group met a single mom who was pregnant—a cashier at her favorite tea shop. She had no support system, so our friend asked our group to host a baby shower for her. We purchased some new items for the woman and also collected gently used baby items from our other friends so that all her needs were met. The shower was lovely; we met at the little tea shop where she worked and had appetizers, dessert, and tea. This young mom was overwhelmed by the generosity of strangers!

# Notes

## Introduction

1. Maria Faustina Kowalska, *Diary: Divine Mercy in My Soul*, 3rd ed. (Stockbridge, MA: Marian Press, 1987), 476. All citations of the *Diary* refer to this edition. The numbers cited correspond to paragraph numbers in the *Diary*.

2. Francis, "Pope Francis: Homily with Announcement of Holy Year of Mercy," Vatican Radio, March 13, 2015, http://en.radiovaticana.va/news/2015/03/13/pope_francis_homily_with_announcement_of_year_of_mercy/1129218.

3. Francis, *Misericordiae Vultus*: Bull of Indiction of the Extraordinary Jubilee of Mercy, April 11, 2015, http://w2.vatican.va/content/francesco/en/apost_letters/documents/papa-francesco_bolla_20150411_misericordiae-vultus.html, 15.

4. Michael E. Gaitley, *Divine Mercy Explained: Keys to the Message and Devotion* (Stockbridge, MA: Marian Press, 2013), 6.

5. Francis, "Angelus," January 11, 2015, Libreria Editrice Vaticana, http://w2.vatican.va/content/francesco/en/angelus/2015/documents/papa-francesco_angelus_20150111.html.

## 1. St. Faustina, Apostle of Divine Mercy

1. According to the website of the Congregation of the Sisters of Our Lady of Mercy, "Although it is neither the first picture painted under Sr. Faustina's direction nor the first image displayed in the chapels of her Congregation, Jesus's will: **I desire that this image be venerated, first in your chapel, and [then] throughout the world** (*Diary* 47) has been fulfilled by means of this picture." http://www.faustyna.pl/zmbm/en/image/.

2. M. Elzbieta Siepak, *A Gift from God for Our Times: The Life and Mission of St. Faustina* (Krakow: Misericordia Publications, 2007), 35.

3. Kowalska, *Diary*, 47–48.

4. Ewa Czackzkowska. *Faustina the Mystic and Her Message* (Stockbridge, MA: Marian Press, 2014), 244.

5. Siepak, *Gift from God for Our Times*, 111–12.

6. John Paul II, *Memory and Identity: Conversations at the Dawn of a Millennium* (New York: Rizzoli, 2005), 54.

7. Benedict XVI, "Regina Caeli Address for Divine Mercy Sunday," April 23, 2006, quoted in "Pope Benedict XVI's Top 10 Mercy Quotes," http://www.thedivinemercy.org/news/story.php?NID=5206&title=Pope-Benedict-XVIs-Top-10-Mercy-Quotes.

8. Francis, "Angelus," March 17, 2013, http://w2.vatican.va/content/francesco/en/angelus/2013/documents/papa-francesco_angelus_20130317.html.

9. The original, unabridged version of this prayer is in Appendix 1.

## 2. Developing Trust in Jesus through the Divine Mercy Devotion

1. Siepak, *A Gift from God for Our Times*, 15–16.

2. Scott Hahn, Curtis Mitch, and Dennis Walters, "Commentary on Luke 6:36," *Ignatius Study Bible: New Testament* (San Francisco: Ignatius Press, 2010), 119.

3. "Pictures vs. Words," SkillsToolbox.com, http://www.skillstoolbox.com/career-and-education-skills/learning-skills/effective-learning-strategies/pictures-vs-words/.

4. Kowalska, *Diary*, 48, 414, 570, 742, and 1789.

5. Gaitley, *Divine Mercy Explained*, 12.

6. These words of Pope John Paul II were related by Dr. Fuster to Fr. Seraphim Michalenko, M.I.C., and published in Michael E. Gaitley, *The Second Greatest Story Ever Told* (Stockbridge, MA: Marian Press, 2015), 78.

7. Gaitley, *Divine Mercy Explained*, 11.

8. Kowalska, *Diary*, 1320.

9. Kowalska, Introduction to the *Diary*, xxv.

## 4. The Corporal Works of Mercy

1. Kowalska, *Diary*, 163.

2. Michael E. Gaitley, *You Did It to Me: A Practical Guide to Mercy in Action* (Stockbridge, MA: Marian Press, 2014), 35.

3. Anup Shah, "Today, Around 21,000 Children Died around the World," *Global Issues: Social, Political, Economic and Environmental Issues That Affect Us All*, http://www.globalissues.org/article/715/today-21000-children-died-around-the-world.

4. Gaitley, *You Did It to Me*, 126–27.

5. New America, Atlas website, "Federal School Nutrition Programs," http://atlas.newamerica.org/federal-school-nutrition-programs.

6. World Health Organization, "Global Health Observatory Data Repository: WORLD: Diarrhoeal Diseases," http://apps.who.int/gho/data/view.main.CM100WORLD-CH3?lang=en.

7. World Health Organization, "Safer Water, Better Health: Costs, Benefits, and Sustainability of Interventions to Protect and Promote Health," http://whqlibdoc.who.int/publications/2008/9789241596435_eng.pdf.

8. Jamil Zaki, "What, Me Care? Young Are Less Empathetic," *Scientific American*, December 23, 2010, http://www.scientificamerican.com/article/what-me-care.

9. Francis, *Misericordiae Vultus*, 19.

10. Ibid., 24.

11. Some suggested places to order from: Marians of the Immaculate Conception at http://www.marian.org/enrollments; Franciscan Friars of the Third Order Regular (my brother is in formation there—your donation will help to support vocations) at http://www.franciscanstor.org/Our_Services/Mass_and_Greeting_Cards; and Trademark Catholic Stationery and Gifts (www.catholicstationery.com).

## 5. The Spiritual Works of Mercy

1. Mother Teresa, *A Simple Path* (New York: Ballantine Books, 1995), 79.

2. Francis, "Meeting with Young People from Argentina from the Apostolic Journey to Rio de Janeiro on the Occasion of the 28th World Youth Day," Thursday, July 25, 2013, http://w2.vatican.va/content/francesco/en/speeches/2013/july/documents/papa-francesco_20130725_gmg-argentini-rio.html.

3. Francis, *The Church of Mercy* (Chicago: Loyola Press, 2014), 11.

4. Pope Francis's homilies, encyclicals, and other writings and speeches are available free online at www.vatican.va.

5. Little Flower Keepsakes. facebook.com/Little-Flower-Keepsakes.

6. John Paul II, "Day of Pardon Mass, March 12, 2000," http://
w2.vatican.va/content/john-paul-ii/en/homilies/2000/docu-
ments/hf_jp-ii_hom_20000312_pardon.html.

## 6. Mary, Mother of Mercy

1. Siepak, *A Gift from God for Our Times*, 39.

2. See John Paul II, *Veritatis Splendor* (1993), 118. http://
w2.vatican.va/content/john-paul-ii/en/encyclicals/documents/
hf_jp-ii_enc_06081993_veritatis-splendor.html.

3. Donald Calloway, *Purest of All Lilies: The Virgin Mary in the
Spirituality of St. Faustina* (Stockbridge, MA: Marian Press, 2010),
54.

4. Louis de Montfort, *True Devotion to Mary* (Rockford, IL: Tan
Books and Publishers, 1941), 96.

5. Francis, "Homily on the Solemnity of the Assumption of
the Blessed Virgin Mary, August 15, 2013," http://w2.vatican.va/
content/francesco/en/homilies/2013/documents/papa-fran-
cesco_20130815_omelia-assunzione.html.

6. Teresa of Ávila, *The Collected Works of St. Teresa of Avila*,
trans. Kieran Kavanaugh and Otilio Rodriguez (Washington, DC:
Institute of Carmelite Studies, 1976), 3:119–20.

7. George Kosicki, *Divine Mercy's Prescription for Spiritual
Health* (Huntington, IN: Our Sunday Visitor, 2002), 95. Used with
permission of the Marians of the Immaculate Conception.

## Appendix 1: Prayers

1. Kosicki, *Divine Mercy's Prescription for Spiritual Health*,
95. Used with permission of the Marians of the Immaculate
Conception.

2. Francis Coomes, S.J., *Mothers' Manual* (Brooklyn, William
J. Hirten Co., Inc, 5th edition), 43–44.

**Michele Faehnle** is a blogger, contributor to *Catholic-Mom.com*, and codirector of the Columbus Catholic Women's Conference. She earned a bachelor of science degree (cum laude) in nursing from Franciscan University of Steubenville in 1999. After twelve years as a labor and delivery nurse, she left nursing to be home with her growing family and answer the call to the New Evangelization. Faehnle has spoken at the National Shrine of Divine Mercy and to several women's groups and conferences, including the annual convention of the Columbus Diocesan Council of Catholic Women. Faehnle also volunteers at her parish and her children's Catholic school. She and her husband, Matthew, have four children and live in Columbus, Ohio.

**Emily Jaminet** is a blogger and contributor to *Catholic-Mom.com*, and serves on the leadership team of the Columbus Catholic Women's Conference. She earned a bachelor's degree in mental health and human services with a minor in human life studies from Franciscan University of Steubenville in 1998. After a brief stint as an administrative assistant at the Pittsburgh Leadership Foundation, a Christian nonprofit, she decided to stay at home with her children.

Jaminet does a daily short segment called "A Mother's Moment" on St. Gabriel Catholic Radio AM 820. She has spoken to several women's groups and conferences, including Zanesville Women's Conference, St. Mary's of Delaware Lenten Women's Reflection, and Women's Day of Reflection for Homeschoolers. Jaminet also volunteers at her parish and her children's Catholic schools. She and her husband, John, have seven children and live in Columbus, Ohio.

# More in the

# CATHOLICMOM.COM

## Book Series

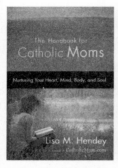

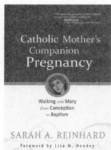

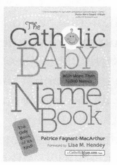

**Available wherever books and eBooks are sold.**
For more information, **visit avemariapress.com.**

**AVE MARIA PRESS**
A Ministry of the United States
Province of Holy Cross